Language 54

Themes 66

Skills and Practice 76

Glossary 94

What are Oxford Literature Companions?

Oxford Literature Companions is a series designed to provide you with comprehensive support for popular set texts. You can use the Companion alongside your novel, using relevant sections during your studies or using the book as a whole for revision.

Each Companion includes detailed guidance and practical activities on:

- **Plot and Structure**
- **Context**
- **Characters**
- **Language**
- **Themes**
- **Skills and Practice**

How does this book help with exam preparation?

As well as providing guidance on key areas of the novel, throughout this book you will also find 'Upgrade' features. These are tips to help with your exam preparation and performance.

In addition, in the extensive **Skills and Practice** chapter, the **Exam skills** section provides detailed guidance on areas such as how to prepare for the exam, understanding the question, planning your response and hints for what to do (or not do) in the exam.

In the **Skills and Practice** chapter there is also a bank of **Sample questions** and **Sample answers**. The **Sample answers** are marked and include annotations and a summative comment.

How does this book help with terminology?

Throughout the book, key terms are **highlighted** in the text and explained on the same page. There is also a detailed **Glossary** at the end of the book that explains, in the context of the novel, all the relevant literary terms highlighted in this book.

How does this book work?

Each book in the Oxford Literature Companions series follows the same approach and includes the following features:

- **Key quotations** from the novel
- **Key terms** explained on the page and linked to a complete glossary at the end of the book
- **Activity boxes** to help improve your understanding of the text
- **Upgrade** tips to help prepare you for your assessment

To help illustrate the features in this book, here are two annotated pages taken from this Oxford Literature Companion:

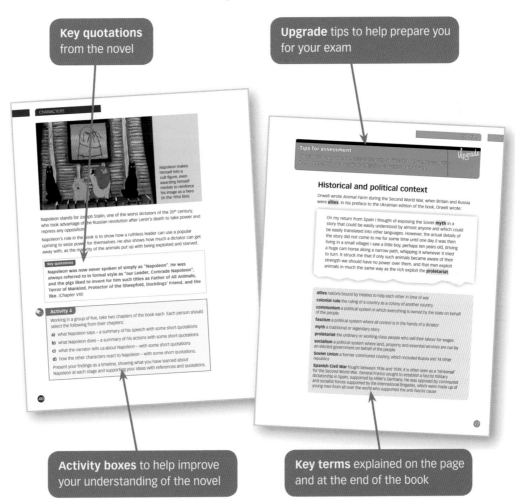

Key quotations from the novel

Upgrade tips to help prepare you for your exam

Activity boxes to help improve your understanding of the novel

Key terms explained on the page and at the end of the book

Plot

Chapter I

Mr Jones is the owner of Manor Farm. Lazy and frequently drunk, he treats the animals badly and sometimes forgets to feed them. One evening, when he hasn't locked up properly, the animals 'agreed that they should all meet in the big barn as soon as Mr Jones was safely out of the way'.

Old Major, the senior boar on the farm, tells them of his dream, giving a long and inspiring speech in which he urges them to rise up against humans and take over the farm for themselves. He outlines certain principles the animals should follow and teaches them a rousing song, which they all join in singing, until Mr Jones 'seized the gun which always stood in a corner of his bedroom, and let fly a charge of Number 6 shot into the darkness'.

- The opening chapter presents the situation at the farm, showing why the animals want to rebel against Mr Jones and outlining the dream.
- Old Major shows the animals the possibility of a different way of running the farm for themselves.
- The chapter introduces many of the characters that play important roles in the rest of the book.
- It demonstrates Orwell's use of rhetoric and an emotional song, 'Beasts of England', in the novel. Many revolutionaries used similar devices to rouse support for their ideas in Russia and elsewhere around the world.
- Old Major's speech outlines the way the animals should run the farm after the Rebellion is successful.

> **Key quotations**
>
> "Man serves the interests of no creature except himself. And among us animals let there be perfect unity, perfect comradeship in the struggle. All men are enemies. All animals are comrades."

Chapter II

Old Major dies soon after his speech, but the animals start secret preparations for the coming of the Rebellion. The pigs teach the others about the principles of **Animalism** as they 'were generally recognised as being the cleverest of the animals'. They have to overcome the belief of some animals that humans are rightfully in charge and the stories of Moses the raven about a place called Sugarcandy Mountain where animals go when they die.

Activity 1

How does Orwell use rhetorical devices to make old Major's speech so convincing? Consider his use of the following:

- repetition of words and/or phrases
- sound patterns (**alliteration**, **assonance**, **onomatopoeia**, etc.)
- contrasts and opposites
- **tripling**
- **rhetorical question**
- **metaphor** and **anecdote**
- the building up of points in a logical order to make an overwhelming case
- inclusive terms such as 'you', 'you and I', 'we', 'friends', 'comrades', etc.
- appeals to the emotions and the intellect of the audience (e.g. 'scream your lives out', 'tyranny of human beings').

Copy the speech and use highlighters and annotation to work out which of these devices Orwell uses. Then write a paragraph on Orwell's use of rhetoric in the speech and how effective you think it is.

---

alliteration the repetition of the same letter or sound in words close to each other, e.g. 'I have had...'

anecdote a short story that illustrates a point, e.g. old Major's story about the 'Beasts of England' song

Animalism the name that Orwell gives to the philosophy underpinning the Rebellion; it corresponds to the terms *Marxism*, *communism* or *socialism*

assonance the repetition of vowel sounds, e.g. '... boil you down for the foxhounds...'

metaphor a comparison of one thing to another to make a description more vivid; a metaphor states that one thing *is* another

onomatopoeia the formation of words that sound like the things they describe

rhetorical questions questions that either do not need an answer or to which the answer is provided immediately by the speaker

tripling grouping points in threes

After losing money, Mr Jones takes to drinking even more and the farm is going rapidly downhill. Instead of harvesting the hay, Mr Jones goes to the pub and his men go out rabbiting.

When the starving animals break into the store shed in search of food and the men drive them out with whips, they turn on the humans and chase them from the farm. The Rebellion has suddenly happened and the animals destroy all the whips and other symbols of oppression.

Left to starve, the animals turn on Jones and force him off the farm (as seen in the 1954 film)

The next day, the farm is rechristened Animal Farm and the pigs, who have learned to read and write, paint the **Seven Commandments** on the barn wall. The pigs milk the cows but, when the animals return from harvesting the hay, 'it was noticed that the milk had disappeared'.

- The pigs are presented as the most intelligent animals, taking the lead and educating themselves and the others.

- It is clear that not everyone supports Animalism – some are still in favour of the old **regime**.

- This chapter demonstrates that rebellion can occur when leaders drive underlings too far and are unaware of the underlings' combined strength.

- Orwell continues to show the importance of symbols through the destruction of whips and other instruments of torture and repression, which symbolize human tyranny, and the re-naming of the farm – a symbol of the new era of freedom and equality.

Sadly, many of the animals cannot read the Seven Commandments on the barn wall

- By the end of the chapter, the pig Napoleon seems to be in command and the vanishing milk is the first sign of inequality. Orwell uses this incident to **foreshadow** what happens later in the story.

> **Key quotations**
>
> **They explained that by their studies of the past three months the pigs had succeeded in reducing the principles of Animalism to seven commandments. These seven commandments would now be inscribed on the wall; they would form an unalterable law by which all the animals on Animal Farm must live for ever after.**

foreshadowing a literary technique where the author includes clues for the reader about what will happen later on

regime an authoritarian government

Seven Commandments these are roughly comparable with the Ten Commandments of the Old Testament and lay down a set of rules for a just society

Activity 2

Work in groups of three to create a debate that reflects the viewpoints Orwell writes about in this chapter. Each person should take on one of the following roles.

- One person should take on the role of a pig who is teaching the concepts of Animalism. You will need to use some ideas from old Major's speech and your own arguments to convince the others that this is the right way forward.

- One person should take on the role of an animal, such as Mollie, who is not convinced about Animalism and thinks that the farm needs humans to organize everything. You should select relevant parts of this chapter and your own arguments to try to convince the others.

- One person should take on the role of Moses the raven. You should use the relevant parts of this chapter and your own knowledge of religious arguments to try to convince the others that your ideas about Sugarcandy Mountain are correct.

Make notes of what you want to say and the most persuasive way in which to say it. You could use rhetorical devices to help you.

Chapter III

The animals succeed in bringing in the best harvest ever in a shorter time than the humans. The pigs use their superior intelligence to assume control and they supervise the hard work of the other animals. They start a literacy programme to educate all the animals but most of them find it too difficult. '[... T]he stupider animals such as the sheep, hens and ducks, were unable to learn the Seven Commandments by heart' so Snowball reduces them to the single **maxim** – "Four legs good, two legs bad".

The animals work with determination, especially Boxer, but they have plenty to eat and Sundays off to rest. On Sundays, there is a flag-raising ceremony with a symbolic flag of a hoof and horn on a green field. This is followed by a meeting to outline work for the next week and vote on resolutions.

Napoleon and Snowball always seem to have opposing ideas. Snowball sets up a lot of committees for the animals, few of which are successful. Napoleon takes away the next two litters of dogs, saying he will educate them himself and 'the rest of the farm soon forgot their existence'. It is also discovered that the pigs are keeping the milk and apples for themselves, but Squealer is sent to explain this to the animals.

- Here, Orwell shows the possibility of a rebellion being a new way of organizing society, where everyone works according to their abilities and shares the benefits.
- He also makes the reader aware of how quickly the most intelligent animals take control and ensure that they have privileges not shared by the other animals.
- We see again the way in which Orwell shows the use of **symbolism** in the flag, since a flag is representative of a nation, and its ceremonial raising.
- Orwell demonstrates how the show of **democracy** – the weekly meetings – is subverted by the pigs, who are the only ones to promote resolutions. He also shows the power struggle between Snowball and Napoleon.
- This is the first time Orwell shows Napoleon using Squealer as a 'spin doctor', using a mixture of **propaganda** and threats to convince the animals of his viewpoint.

> **Key quotations**
>
> But everyone worked according to his capacity. The hens and ducks, for instance, saved five bushels of corn at the harvest by gathering up the stray grains. Nobody stole, nobody grumbled over his rations, the quarrelling and biting and jealousy which had been normal features of life in the old days had almost disappeared. Nobody shirked – or almost nobody.

Activity 3

1. Working with a partner, look closely at Squealer's speech near the end of the chapter. Analyse the techniques he uses to convince the other animals that milk and apples should be kept for the pigs. Consider the following:

   - Squealer's use of **false logic**: Why do only the pigs need to be healthy?
   - references to science that are not supported by evidence
   - vague threats about Jones coming back
   - any other techniques you can see.

2. This is the turning point in the Rebellion, when the pigs demand privileges. Why do you think the other animals let them get away with it?

3. What does this show about the way in which Orwell presents the techniques of propaganda? Write a brief analysis of Squealer's manipulation of the truth in this speech.

democracy a system of government that allows everyone to express their views

false logic statements that appear to be logical on the surface, but do not stand up to examination

maxim a saying that is connected to a truth about life or a rule about behaviour

propaganda the deliberate spreading of ideas or information that promote the interests of a particular group

symbolism using objects to represent an idea, e.g. a flag has symbolic meaning as the representation of a country

Chapter IV

News of the Rebellion spreads around the neighbourhood, thanks to the pigeons. Animals on other farms learn 'Beasts of England' and the humans are worried when 'a wave of rebelliousness ran through the countryside'. Jones and his two neighbouring farmers launch an attack on Animal Farm, resulting in the Battle of the Cowshed. Thanks to Snowball's tactics, the animals are victorious and the humans driven out, with the loss of one sheep.

The animals celebrate their victory, bury the sheep and create medals for Animal Hero, First Class and Second Class. Mr Jones's gun is set up by the flagpole for ceremonial firings. After discussion the fight 'was named the Battle of the Cowshed, since that was where the ambush had been sprung'.

- Orwell shows the power of ideas and the ways in which they are spread.
- A well-organized group of underlings is shown to prevail over the privileged group, which continues to underestimate the underlings' power.

- The heroism of Snowball and Boxer is emphasized here to make what happens to them later in the story even more shocking.
- The relationship between Mr Jones, Mr Pilkington and Mr Frederick is introduced and will be significant later in the novel.
- Orwell uses the symbolism and trappings of war (flags, medals, artillery salutes) to make a **satirical** point about a minor skirmish in a farmyard.

> **satirical** in which humour or exaggeration is used to show the vices, follies, abuses and shortcomings of a person or thing

Key quotations

Above all, the tune and even the words of 'Beasts of England' were known everywhere. It had spread with astonishing speed. The human beings could not contain their rage when they heard this song, though they pretended to think it merely ridiculous. They could not understand, they said, how even animals could bring themselves to sing such contemptible rubbish. Any animal caught singing it was given a flogging on the spot. And yet the song was irrepressible. The blackbirds whistled it in the hedges, the pigeons cooed it in the elms, it got into the din of the smithies and the tune of the church bells. And when the human beings listened to it they secretly trembled, hearing in it a prophecy of their future doom.

Activity 4

1. Work with a partner and look at paragraphs 2 and 3 of this chapter. Then do the following:

   a) Find two or three phrases that describe Foxwood.

   b) Find two or three phrases that describe Mr Pilkington.

   c) Find two or three phrases that describe Pinchfield.

   d) Find two or three phrases that describe Mr Frederick.

2. What do you think it suggests about them that the initials of the farms and their owners are FP and PF? Do you think their names suggest that Foxwood belongs to a hunter and Pinchfield to a miser? How does Orwell convey the differences between these neighbours and their farms?

3. How does Orwell show the farmers coming together? In what ways does he show their reactions to the Rebellion?

4. How does his use of language reveal the farmers' increasing desperation at the Rebellion's success?

5. Write two or three paragraphs commenting on the way in which Orwell uses language effectively and economically to show the attitudes of other farmers to Animal Farm.

Chapter V

Mollie deserts Animal Farm and goes over to the humans. The rivalry between Napoleon and Snowball continues and grows: 'These two disagreed at every point where disagreement was possible.'

Finally, it comes to a head. Snowball has been working on plans for a windmill to produce electricity which, he says, will greatly reduce the animals' work and provide comfort in their accommodation. Napoleon is opposed to the windmill and, when it is debated, Napoleon turns his trained dogs on Snowball and drives him from the farm.

Napoleon then 'announced that from now on the Sunday-morning Meetings would come to an end'. These are to be replaced by orders from the pigs. Objections are faced down by the dogs and sheep, and Squealer explains why the new system will work better. Napoleon also announces that the windmill will be built after all and Squealer explains that it was all Napoleon's idea originally.

- This chapter shows the differences in ideas between Snowball, who seeks agreement for his plans, and Napoleon, who imposes his through violence.
- Orwell shows that even those who are clever and articulate can be defeated by violence.
- Orwell demonstrates how power can be seized from the majority. It is obvious that Napoleon has planned this from the beginning in his training of the dogs and the sheep.
- Towards the end of the chapter, the new social division is shown through the physical division in the barn. The pigs sit on a higher platform and the rest of the animals sit facing them on the floor.

Key quotations

Napoleon, with the dogs following him, now mounted onto the raised portion of the floor where Major had previously stood to deliver his speech. He announced that from now on the Sunday-morning Meetings would come to an end. They were unnecessary, he said, and wasted time. In future all questions relating to the working of the farm would be settled by a special committee of pigs, presided over by himself. These would meet in private and afterwards communicate their decisions to the others. The animals would still assemble on Sunday mornings to salute the flag, sing 'Beasts of England' and receive their orders for the week; but there would be no more debates.

Activity 5

1. Work with a partner and look closely at Orwell's use of language in this chapter.

   a) Find three phrases that tell us that Snowball was a clever thinker.

   b) Find three phrases that show Snowball was a persuasive speaker.

   c) Find three phrases that demonstrate Napoleon's lack of the above skills.

   d) Find three phrases that show the use of violence (as demonstrated by Napoleon) overcoming democratic debate (as demonstrated by Snowball).

2. Now write two or three paragraphs that analyse how the phrases you have chosen are effective in showing the ways in which creative thinking can be overcome by brute force.

Chapter VI

The animals work harder than ever to build the windmill, at the expense of the harvest, which means the farm is less productive. They are told that the 'needs of the windmill must override everything else'. Napoleon announces that he is employing Whymper, a solicitor, in order to trade for necessary supplies that cannot be produced on the farm.

Then the pigs move into the farmhouse. This makes the other animals uneasy, especially as the pigs sleep in the beds.

The pigs, led by Napoleon, become accustomed to the creature comforts in the farmhouse (in the 1954 film)

The windmill is partly built and the animals are proud of their achievement. Then the mill is destroyed by a violent storm. Napoleon declares its destruction to be the work of Snowball: **"this traitor has crept here under cover of night and destroyed our work of nearly a year"**. Napoleon offers a reward for Snowball's death or capture.

- This chapter shows the pigs moving away from the principles of Animalism and Napoleon further establishing his authority.

- It seems that, whenever the pigs want to do something forbidden, the commandments are changed from those the animals remember. Orwell is showing how a subtle alteration can change the meaning of a law to suit those in power.

- The pigs are shown to take advantage of the other animals' willingness to work hard, summed up in Boxer's two **slogans**.

- This chapter highlights the difficulties of being self-sufficient without the necessary tools or skills, making the need for trade essential.

Key quotations

There would be no need for any of the animals to come in contact with human beings, which would clearly be most undesirable. He intended to take the whole burden upon his own shoulders. A Mr Whymper, a solicitor living in Willingdon, had agreed to act as intermediary between Animal Farm and the outside world, and would visit the farm every Monday morning to receive his instructions.

---

slogan a motto expressing the aims of a group

Activity 6

Working with a partner, examine the extract that begins 'Napoleon paced to and fro in silence...' to the end of Chapter VI.

1. Discuss how Orwell conveys the impression of a theatrical performance from Napoleon here. Consider what he says and the way he acts in this extract. Look at the following phrases:

   - 'snuffing at the ground'

   - 'suddenly roared'

   - 'shocked beyond measure'

   - 'thinking out ways of catching Snowball'

   - 'pronounced them to be Snowball's'.

2. How does Napoleon use both fear and bribery to help persuade the animals?

3. Write a paragraph about the way Orwell uses language to suggest one thing to the reader while the animals are given a different idea. How can the reader see it as a performance, while the animals believe it is real?

Chapter VII

The rebuilding of the windmill is harder than ever because of a long, bitter winter. Food runs low and the animals are close to starving, but 'it was vitally necessary to conceal this fact from the outside world.'

Napoleon negotiates to sell timber to the two neighbouring farms. The hens rebel when told that they must send their eggs to market to buy food, so Napoleon starves them into surrender.

He then sends Squealer to announce that Snowball had been in league with Mr Jones all along. This is a step too far even for Boxer, but Napoleon stages a hideous scene of public confession and slaughter that leaves the animals shaken and miserable. When they sing 'Beasts of England' for comfort, they are told that 'by a special decree of Comrade Napoleon, "Beasts of England" had been abolished'.

- This chapter shows the principles of the Rebellion deteriorating.
- Orwell demonstrates the way in which any dissent is put down by a ruthless leader.
- Orwell also conveys how propaganda can be self-defeating when taken too far. Squealer has got away with his lies and manipulation so far, but even Boxer refuses to believe that Snowball was in league with Jones.

> **Key quotations**
>
> When it was all over, the remaining animals, except for the pigs and dogs, crept away in a body. They were shaken and miserable. They did not know which was more shocking – the treachery of the animals who had leagued themselves with Snowball, or the cruel retribution they had just witnessed. In the old days there had often been scenes of bloodshed equally terrible, but it seemed to all of them that it was far worse now that it was happening among themselves.

Activity 7

1. Copy out Clover's thoughts after the executions. How does Orwell use negative structures to show what the animals had hoped for ('it was not...')?

2. Try rewriting these as positive structures. For example, **'this was not what they had aimed at when they had set themselves years ago to work for the overthrow of the human race'** would become 'what they had hoped for when they set themselves to work for the overthrow of the human race was...'.

3. Why do you think Orwell has chosen to express Clover's thoughts using negative structures? Annotate your copy with your ideas.

Chapter VIII

Napoleon becomes more like a dictator than ever. 'Confessions', executions and rumours continue. 'Beasts of England' is replaced by a poem praising Comrade Napoleon: 'It was surmounted by a portrait of Napoleon, in profile, executed by Squealer in white paint.' Napoleon tries to play Frederick and Pilkington off against each other over the sale of timber. He is defrauded by Frederick, who pays him in forged banknotes and then launches a full-scale attack on Animal Farm, blowing up the windmill.

The animals drive Frederick and his men from the farm at heavy cost, including the destruction of the windmill. However, Napoleon treats this as a great victory. Subsequently, 'in the general rejoicings the unfortunate affair of the bank-notes was forgotten'. The pigs find a case of whisky and get very drunk. In spite of a bad hangover the next day, Napoleon decides to plant barley.

The windmill represented the long hours of toil the animals put into trying to bring electricity and a more comfortable life to the farm – all destroyed (in the 1999 film)

- This chapter shows the expansion of Napoleon's ambition to his neighbours as he tries to manipulate them.

- The replacing of a song that glorifies freedom and community with one that praises an individual leader is shown by Orwell to be part of Napoleon's cult of personality and represents a further erosion of the ideals of Animalism.

- Orwell demonstrates the animals' vulnerability in the face of superior arms and ruthlessness.

- The propaganda spread by Squealer is still believed because the animals have no other source of information. Orwell shows how knowledge gives power to those who have it and how it is easy to exploit those without it.

Key quotations

They had won, but they were weary and bleeding. Slowly they began to limp back towards the farm. The sight of their dead comrades stretched upon the grass moved some of them to tears. And for a little while they halted in sorrowful silence at the place where the windmill had once stood. Yes, it was gone, almost the last trace of their labour was gone! Even the foundations were partially destroyed. And in rebuilding it they could not this time, as before, make use of the fallen stones. This time the stones had vanished too. The force of the explosion had flung them to distances of hundreds of yards. It was as though the windmill had never been.

Activity 8

Work with a partner.

1. Re-read the two paragraphs from 'At about the same time it was given out that Napoleon had arranged to sell the pile of timber to Mr Pilkington...' to 'Squealer was soon able to convince them that their memories had been at fault'.

    a) Make a list of the atrocities alleged against Mr Frederick.

    b) Make a list of the crimes alleged against Snowball.

2. What are the animals' reactions to these allegations? What do you think Orwell is saying about the nature of propaganda?

3. One of you should rewrite the allegations against Frederick as a series of Twitter feeds; the other should react as the animals might and tweet their replies.

4. Write two or three paragraphs on how Orwell shows that rumours and propaganda keep the pigs in control.

Chapter IX

The next winter is just as hard: 'Once again all rations were reduced except those of the pigs and the dogs.' There are now 31 more piglets, sired by Napoleon. There are more processions and ceremonies. Moses reappears on the farm after several years' absence.

Boxer works untiringly, but a month before his retirement, he collapses. Squealer announces that Boxer will be taken to the vet to be cured. However, when the van arrives, Benjamin announces that it is from the horse slaughterer. Boxer is taken away to be killed. Squealer convinces the animals that Boxer was given the best hospital treatment and died anyway. 'The animals were enormously relieved to hear this.' The pigs buy another case of whisky.

- This chapter shows the pigs' contempt for Boxer, the most willing hard worker on the farm.

- Orwell demonstrates the total lack of equality that now prevails at Animal Farm.

- Orwell shows how the animals accept what they are told because their old lives at Manor Farm are now so far in the past.

- Orwell demonstrates the new acceptance of Moses the raven, Mr Jones's former pet, which foreshadows what happens at the end of the book.

Key quotations

All the animals took up the cry of "Get out, Boxer, get out!" But the van was already gathering speed and drawing away from them. It was uncertain whether Boxer had understood what Clover had said. But a moment later his face disappeared from the window and there was the sound of a tremendous drumming of hoofs inside the van. He was trying to kick his way out. The time had been when a few kicks from Boxer's hoofs would have smashed the van to matchwood. But alas! his strength had left him; and in a few moments the sound of drumming hoofs grew fainter and died away.

Activity 9

Working with a partner or in a small group, re-read the section of this chapter where Orwell describes the return of Moses the raven. Complete the following tasks.

1. What kind of human character might Moses represent and what do you think the purpose of Sugarcandy Mountain could be?

2. Why do you think the pigs allowed him back, when they didn't believe what he said?

3. If Moses represents a religious leader, how do the animals' differing reactions to him reflect the ways that people regard religion and the promises it makes?

4. 'Religion is the sigh of the oppressed creature, the heart of a heartless world, and the soul of soulless conditions. It is the opium of the people' (Karl Marx). Discuss how true you think this is with regard to the animals' situation in the novel.

5. Write a pamphlet for other students about the role of Moses in the novel. You could use illustrations, bullet points, headings, etc. to structure your pamphlet.

Chapter X

As the years pass, more animals die and new ones are born or bought. For most 'the Rebellion was only a dim tradition, passed on by word of mouth'. Animal Farm becomes prosperous, although only the pigs and dogs benefit.

The pigs start walking on two legs and carrying whips. They make peace with their human neighbours, who are all impressed with the hard work and the low rations given to the farm animals. The last betrayal is Napoleon's announcement that 'Henceforward the farm was to be known as "The Manor Farm" – which, he believed, was its correct and original name.' The sound of furious arguing brings the animals to the farmhouse windows, but when they peer in they cannot tell the men from the pigs.

- Orwell uses this chapter to show how a revolution not only replaces a regime but often becomes just like the regime it replaces.
- The chapter draws together the idea that those who seize power, even by democratic means, use it to suppress others.
- It demonstrates how completely power corrupts, as those who start with ideals quickly become corrupt in their actions and their language.

In the 1954 film, Benjamin can see that the pigs are turning into humans

---

Key quotations

Twelve voices were shouting in anger, and they were all alike. No question, now, what had happened to the faces of the pigs. The creatures outside looked from pig to man, and from man to pig, and from pig to man again: but already it was impossible to say which was which.

Activity 10

Working with a partner, discuss how the phrases below from Chapter X echo other phrases in Chapter I. Write down the pairs of equivalent phrases from Chapters I and X. Why do you think Orwell has used this technique?

> **Key quotations**
>
> But still, neither pigs nor dogs produced any food by their own labour; and there were very many of them, and their appetites were always good.
>
> As for the others, their life, so far as they knew, was as it had always been. They were generally hungry, they slept on straw, they drank from the pool, they laboured in the fields; in winter they were troubled by the cold, and in summer by the flies.
>
> If they went hungry, it was not from feeding tyrannical human beings; if they worked hard, at least they worked for themselves. No creature among them went upon two legs. No creature called any other creature "Master". All animals were equal.
>
> Henceforward the farm was to be known as "The Manor Farm" – which, he believed, was its correct and original name.

Write your conclusions in the form of revision notes.

Tips for assessment

When writing about Orwell's plot and structure, it is important to include the idea of the circular outline of the novel. The whole point is that it supports Orwell's idea that violent revolution merely leads to another oppression in the end. If your exam board assesses context, then you can apply this to the Russian revolution, which replaced the Tsar with Stalin.

Structure

By setting his story on a farm, Orwell is able to keep the setting within a defined boundary, which reflects the frontiers of a country or state. The neighbouring farms represent states that share borders.

The story also has a circular structure. It begins with the oppression of farm animals by the humans in charge of them and ends with their oppression by a class of animals who have become more like humans. In between, Orwell shows the possibilities of a community built on equality and tolerance and how it is slowly destroyed by those who are clever and ruthless. Once we see the pigs keep the milk and apples for themselves, we know it is only a matter of time before they take more and more privileges.

Most novels have a three-act structure, which consists of an inciting incident (the event that triggers the rest of the plot), a climax (the event that everything in the novel has been building towards) and a resolution (the way everything is tied up at the end). Orwell's novel also follows this pattern.

In *Animal Farm* the inciting incident is the Rebellion, since without the motivation of hunger and injustice to drive them, it is unlikely that old Major's ideas would have been acted upon. The climax is the death of Boxer, since it reveals the distance the rulers have come from the principles of equality and freedom that started the Rebellion. The resolution is the animals' realization that there is no difference between the pigs and the humans – between one set of oppressors and the other.

Throughout the book, Orwell builds a series of incidents that lead to the final scene. The incidents are documented by the gradual altering of the Seven Commandments of Animalism. Each time the pigs take more power and privilege, the commandments are altered to fit. It is the inevitability of the way the pigs progress towards becoming human that gives the novel structure, as well as the incidents that mirror one another – the destruction of the windmill, the two battles and the killing of those animals who speak out or lose their usefulness. The behaviour of the pigs mirrors the behaviour of the humans.

The structure of *Animal Farm* is shaped by Orwell's crafting of the following incidents in the novel:

- By the end of Chapter III, the milk and apples are reserved for the pigs alone, Napoleon has taken nine puppies to 'educate' them himself and Squealer has been established as the pigs' propagandist. These are early examples of Orwell's foreshadowing of the separation of the pigs as a privileged class.

- There is a time of total solidarity when the animals fight against the humans in the Battle of the Cowshed, led mainly by Snowball. This shows what is possible and creates a contrast with what happens afterwards. Orwell shows that it is feasible to create a society based on equality. It foreshadows the Battle of the Windmill, which is much more hard fought by a society that is no longer equal.

- Chapter V shows dissension growing on the farm as animals take sides for Snowball or Napoleon over the windmill. The verbal debate is won by Snowball, but Napoleon uses aggression, in the shape of the dogs, to win power and get rid of Snowball. He promptly ends the meetings and democratic votes, using a mixture of fear and propaganda to stop any rebellion. When he decrees the windmill will be built, nobody argues against him. The dogs tip the balance of power and make it impossible for the farm to operate as a democracy.

- Next, the pigs start trading with humans and then move into the farmhouse, where they use the beds. This is not only against the commandments; it shows the further separation of the pigs and the dogs from the rest of the animals – just like a **class system**. When the windmill is destroyed by a storm, Napoleon uses the incident to blacken Snowball further. This incident also foreshadows the destruction of the second windmill – this time deliberately – by Frederick.

- The hard weather and time spent on the windmill mean that food is scarce for the farm animals. When the hens rebel against giving up their eggs for sale, Napoleon starves them into submission. Every bad thing that happens is laid at Snowball's door until the animals are convinced he is their sworn enemy. This is followed by a show trial and the slaughter of many animals accused of helping Snowball, which gets rid of Napoleon's opposition under the pretence of necessary security and breaks one of the commandments. Finally the singing of 'Beasts of England' is prohibited. This shows the **idealism** of the Rebellion being cast aside.

- Napoleon establishes himself as dictator or 'Leader' in a way that glorifies him over all the other animals – much as the humans on the adjoining farms. He tries to play off his human neighbours against each other. This results in the Battle of the Windmill and its destruction. The pigs find a case of whisky and get very drunk, thereby breaking another of the commandments and repeating the behaviour of Jones at the start of the story.

- In Chapter IX, life gets even harder for most of the animals. There are more pigs and dogs to feed and the windmill to be replaced. Napoleon declares Animal Farm a republic and is elected president unopposed. He takes the animals' minds off their suffering by holding regular parades and ceremonies. When Boxer falls ill through overwork, instead of the promised retirement, he is sold to the **knacker** and taken away. The pigs buy another case of whisky with the money. These actions, like Napoleon's previous ones, all go directly against old Major's principles.

- In the final chapter, the pigs behave exactly like the human beings they fought to **depose** at the beginning of the book. Their betrayal of Animalism is complete. They have broken the final commandment and replaced all the commandments with a single statement that makes nonsense of Animalism and language alike.

class system a way of grouping people according to birth, income or education

depose remove from power forcibly

idealism believing in high ideals and noble goals

knacker a person who buys and slaughters horses and then sells the meat, bones and hides

You should think about cause and effect in the structure of a novel. That is, the way one action, or set of actions, leads to another. For example, the fact that the pigs are clever gives them the edge over the other animals. When they see how their leadership is accepted, this encourages them to use their power more. Conversely, when the other animals feel something is wrong, they do not have the confidence to stand together against it, which makes it harder to do so the next time too, and so on.

Tips for assessment

You will need to show that you have understood *how* Orwell has structured
the novel and *why* he has chosen this structure. For example, it is not enough
to say the pigs start breaking the commandments. You must relate this to the
way they abandon old Major's principles, the way in which they take power and
privilege for themselves, and what this means for the animals.

Viewpoint

The novel uses an **omniscient narrator**, which makes it easy for Orwell to show
different viewpoints. The first chapter, for example, is written mostly from the
viewpoint of old Major as he makes his speech, whereas Chapter II is seen at least
in part from the pigs' point of view as they try to educate the others. This makes it
possible for the narrator to move around between the characters. For the most part,
the narrator sees things from the viewpoint of the common animals, while not being
one of them, which gives an emotional distance but also creates empathy in the
reader.

When Orwell uses the **passive voice**, as in 'it was noticed that the milk had
disappeared' *(Chapter II)*, we assume that it's the animals who notice, but they
don't seem to comprehend that this is the pigs' doing. This technique is used by
Orwell to demonstrate the difference between the reader, who understands what is
going on, and the animals, who don't.

Activity 11

1. Copy out the Seven Commandments, leaving a space underneath each one.
   In each space, write how and when the commandment is broken. Add the
   changes to each commandment, as made by Squealer, in a different colour.

2. What happens to the commandments at the end of the novel? What do you
   think Orwell wanted to show by their replacement with a single nonsense
   statement?

3. How is the slogan **"Four legs good, two legs bad"** *(Chapter III)* altered by
   Squealer in Chapter X and why?

4. Write a short article of about 250 words for a student literary magazine,
   based on your findings, showing how Orwell uses the framework of the Seven
   Commandments to trace the corruption of Animalism and the expansion
   of power by the pigs. You should include references and quotations where
   appropriate.

omniscient narrator a narrator who knows the thoughts and feelings of all the characters and can tell the story from multiple viewpoints

passive voice this is the opposite of the active voice and focuses on the thing rather than the action, e.g. 'it was noticed' rather than 'the animals noticed'

Activity 12

1. Look through the bullet points on pages 22–23. Discuss how Orwell uses the following techniques to help structure the novel:

   a) foreshadowing

   b) mirroring (i.e. repeating similar events).

2. In what ways do you think Orwell makes it inevitable that the pigs would turn into humans at the end of the book? You should consider the ways in which the pigs take privileges, the lack of protest from the animals, the way the story of the Rebellion is rewritten, the construction of an elaborate lie about Snowball and the use of the dogs and sheep.

3. What point do you think Orwell is making by giving his novel a circular structure, so that it begins with oppression by Mr Jones on Manor Farm and ends with oppression by Napoleon on Manor Farm?

4. Use your findings to create a timeline showing how Orwell has structured the novel. You could illustrate it if you wish.

Writing about plot and structure

Upgrade

You need to know *Animal Farm* very thoroughly. Although you may not be questioned directly on the plot of the novel, you need to show that you understand all the key events and why they happen. This doesn't mean you should tell the story, but that you should be able to select events that are relevant to the question.

Remember to use evidence from the text. Your answer should contain a mixture of references and direct quotations. For example, when writing about the structure of the book, you should include the idea of how all the points made by old Major in his speech were first used as the basis for Animalism and then gradually abandoned as power corrupts the leaders.

Biography of George Orwell

- George Orwell was born Eric Arthur Blair in the state of Bihar, India in 1903. He was educated as a King's Scholar at Eton, where he edited a school newspaper. Orwell's experiences at Eton made him very aware of how the class system worked to the benefit of the rich. He shows this in the way the humans – and later the pigs – behave towards the animals on the farm.

- In 1922, he joined the Imperial Burma police but became unhappy with Britain's imperial role and, in 1927, he resigned in order to write. Orwell saw the effects of **colonial rule** and the way it oppressed the people whose land had been taken over. He used these feelings in his depiction of Mr Jones and then Napoleon, each of whom effectively takes over and oppresses the animals.

- In 1928, he moved to Paris where he lived and wrote for two years before returning to London. His experiences were later published as *Down and Out in Paris and London.*

George Orwell's most famous novels were *1984* and *Animal Farm*

- In the next few years, Orwell taught and wrote, publishing novels and writing articles for magazines and newspapers. He also developed a strong social conscience, which shaped his writing in books such as *The Road to Wigan Pier*. This is shown in the way the ordinary animals suffer from overwork and hunger on the farm.

- In 1936, Orwell married Eileen O'Shaugnessy and then went to fight in the **Spanish Civil War** on the **communist** side. His experiences led to the attitudes later expressed in *Animal Farm* and his most famous novel *1984*. The way in which the **Soviet Union**-backed communist faction spread lies and propaganda about the **socialist** faction, which Orwell was fighting with, both supposedly on the same side against **fascism**, can be seen in the speeches and actions of Squealer.

- During the Second World War, he worked for the BBC and the *Observer*, among other newspapers and magazines, while at the same time writing *Animal Farm*. He and his wife adopted a baby son, Richard. However, Eileen died during an operation in 1945, shortly before *Animal Farm* was published.

- Orwell's health had always been poor and he was diagnosed with tuberculosis while working on *1984*. Following the success of *Animal Farm*, he was swamped with work and wrote many articles and essays. He married Sonia Brownell on his deathbed.

- George Orwell died in 1950 leaving one of the most influential legacies of any British writer.

You should only make reference to the author's life if it is relevant to something in the text or helps to explain his intentions in writing *Animal Farm*.

Historical and political context

Orwell wrote *Animal Farm* during the Second World War, when Britain and Russia were **allies**. In his preface to the Ukrainian edition of the book, Orwell wrote:

> On my return from Spain I thought of exposing the Soviet **myth** in a story that could be easily understood by almost anyone and which could be easily translated into other languages. However, the actual details of the story did not come to me for some time until one day (I was then living in a small village) I saw a little boy, perhaps ten years old, driving a huge cart-horse along a narrow path, whipping it whenever it tried to turn. It struck me that if only such animals became aware of their strength we should have no power over them, and that men exploit animals in much the same way as the rich exploit the **proletariat**.

allies nations bound by treaties to help each other in time of war

colonial rule the ruling of a country as a colony of another country

communism a political system in which everything is owned by the state on behalf of the people

fascism a political system where all control is in the hands of a dictator

myth a traditional or legendary story

proletariat the ordinary or working-class people who sell their labour for wages

socialism a political system where land, property and essential services are run by an elected government on behalf of the people

Soviet Union a former communist country, which included Russia and 14 other republics

Spanish Civil War fought between 1936 and 1939, it is often seen as a 'rehearsal' for the Second World War. General Franco sought to establish a fascist military dictatorship in Spain, supported by Hitler's Germany. He was opposed by communist and socialist forces supported by the International Brigades, which were made up of young men from all over the world who supported the anti-fascist cause

The Russian revolution

Karl Marx wrote his famous 'Communist Manifesto' and Vladimir Lenin used its principles in Russia. It outlines proposals for a communist state where all land and the means of production are owned by the state, governed by the workers. Such a state requires an uprising to overthrow the ruling class and the land and factory owners. This idea was popular with a large number of people living in poverty and oppression under the last Tsar of Russia. It corresponds to old Major's speech to the animals.

This statue of Karl Marx, in Moscow, shows that he is still revered by many people

Activity 1

1. Find a summary of the 'Communist Manifesto' in an encyclopaedia or online and summarize it in ten main points.

2. Read old Major's speech and summarize it in ten main points.

3. Discuss the similarities and differences you notice between these two **ideologies**. Compare your ideas with others in the class.

Tsar Nicholas II took Russia into the First World War and then managed it so badly that he lost millions of men. In 1917, the people rose up against the ruling class in the Russian revolution, led by Lenin. In *Animal Farm*, the Rebellion where Jones is driven from the farm is the **counterpart** to this. In Russia, the revolution was followed by a civil war between Lenin's Bolsheviks and the forces of the Tsar, which was won by the Bolsheviks – later the Communist Party. The country became the Union of Soviet Socialist Republics (USSR). In *Animal Farm*, this is mirrored in the Battle of the Cowshed: 'And so within five minutes of their invasion they were in ignominious retreat by the same way as they had come, with a flock of geese hissing after them and pecking at their calves all the way.' *(Chapter IV)*

When Lenin died in 1924, there was a power struggle between Joseph Stalin and Leon Trotsky, which was eventually won by Stalin. Trotsky was forced into exile. In 1936, it was claimed that Trotsky had plotted against Stalin and many of his 'supporters' were executed or imprisoned. Trotsky himself was murdered by the **KGB** in Mexico in 1940. These are the events on which Napoleon's expulsion and later blackening of Snowball are based.

Stalin soon gained total control, built on:

- a cult of personality, just as Napoleon eventually becomes "Our Leader, Comrade Napoleon" *(Chapter VII)*

- a series of five-year plans which set impossible goals, just like the building and rebuilding of the windmill
- a reign of terror implemented by the KGB, Stalin's secret police force, on which Napoleon's dogs are based

СТЕРЕТЬ С ЛИЦА ЗЕМЛИ ВРАГА НАРОДА ТРОЦКОГО И ЕГО КРОВАВУЮ ФАШИСТСКУЮ ШАЙКУ!

This 1937 poster is an example of the propaganda against Trotsky – it says 'Destroy the Enemy of the People!'

- an absolute state – the secret police rooted out any 'disloyalty' and the state controlled the sources of information, just as Squealer is the only source of information for the animals. Ironically the state newspaper was called *Pravda*, which means 'truth'
- all land and industry being owned by the state; those who objected were killed or sent to work camps (gulags). Stalin is estimated to have killed around 20 million people. This is reflected in Napoleon's executions of the animals.

Stalin's dealings with other countries are reflected in Napoleon's relationships with the neighbouring farms. In 1939, Stalin signed a **non-aggression pact** with Hitler, which was broken in 1941 when Germany invaded the Soviet Union. The Battle of the Windmill is the equivalent in the novel. Stalin later signed a deal with the USA to provide raw materials in exchange for arms, which is similar to Napoleon's deal with Pilkington. When Stalin, Roosevelt and Churchill met at the Tehran Conference in 1943 to discuss strategy for winning the Second World War, there was much disagreement between them, just as **'There were shoutings, bangings on the table, sharp suspicious glances, furious denials'** (*Chapter X*) at the end of the novel.

counterpart person or thing which corresponds to or has the same function as another

ideologies the sets of ideas and beliefs of groups or political parties

KGB *Komitet gosudarstvennoy bezopasnosti*, the state security force, used by Stalin as his secret police

non-aggression pact a treaty between countries agreeing not to go to war with each other but to settle any differences peaceably

Activity 2

Create a PowerPoint presentation to show the main events of the Russian revolution of 1917 and the events that followed it (up to the Treaty of Tehran in 1943). You should include the following:

- bullet point summaries of the most important happenings and people
- pictures and photographs of people and events where possible
- videos of events if you can find them, e.g. Soviet soldiers, Russian peasants, etc.

Try to relate each historical event to its equivalent event in *Animal Farm*. Remember to include references and quotations from the novel in your presentation.

Your presentation should be between five and ten minutes long.

Social context

Following the **Wall Street crash** of 1929, both America and Europe suffered from the Great Depression. This was a period of very high unemployment and poverty for millions of people. In Britain, the effect on heavy industry (shipbuilding, coalmining and steel production) was severe and 22% of the workforce were unemployed. Many people admired the Soviet Union, believing Stalin's propaganda about agricultural production, when in fact millions of peasants starved to death. In the novel, this is shown when 'Napoleon was well aware of the bad results that might follow if the real facts of the food situation were known, and he decided to make use of Mr Whymper to spread a contrary impression.' *(Chapter VII)* It was against this background that Orwell wrote *Animal Farm*. Trade during the Great Depression was difficult as the value of currency plummeted, especially in the Weimar Republic in Germany. This is reflected in the worthless banknotes paid by Frederick for the timber he takes from Animal Farm.

Stalin's propaganda told a story of success in industry and agriculture

Wall Street crash a devastating stock market crash in 1929, which signalled the beginning of the Great Depression

Class inequality

Of course, not everybody suffered equally in the Great Depression. Many of the upper classes and the rich continued to have an affluent and comfortable lifestyle, while the working and middle classes bore the brunt of the unemployment and hardship. In Britain, the country was divided, with the industrial and mining areas in the north and in Wales being extremely poor, while the Midlands and south-east flourished. As Orwell presents it in the novel, 'Rations, reduced in December, were reduced again in February, and lanterns in the stalls were forbidden to save oil. But the pigs seemed comfortable enough, and in fact were putting on weight if anything.' *(Chapter IX)*

British society was also split by its class system, mainly seen in terms of education. As Orwell had observed at Eton, those who could afford private schools saw themselves as natural rulers – like the humans in *Animal Farm* – while many of the working class went to local elementary schools and left at 14 years old. Orwell was very conscious of this social injustice and how it often led to the rise of fascist and communist parties as working people became conscious of being exploited and oppressed by the ruling classes. The pigs and dogs represent the favoured classes on Animal Farm, while the common animals represent the working class. In Russia, the vast majority of people were peasants who worked on small farms and the literacy rate under the Tsar was around 30%. In Britain, the Worker's Educational Association tried to improve opportunities for working-class adults, while the Soviet Union made universal education available to all, just as the pigs initially set about trying to educate the other animals in the novel.

Activity 3

A class system is when society is divided into a hierarchy of groups according to birth, wealth, education or other factors.

1. Working in a small group, decide how you would divide Animal Farm into a class system:

   a) at the start of the novel

   b) after the Battle of the Cowshed

   c) after the expulsion of Snowball

   d) after the Battle of the Windmill

   e) at the end of the novel.

2. What changes have you decided on? On what evidence did you base your decisions?

3. Create a graph or chart to show your findings and surround it with references and quotations as well as your own comments. Share it with the rest of the class.

In the preface to the Ukrainian edition of the book, Orwell summarized the difference, as he saw it, between Britain and the Soviet Union:

> Yet one must remember that England is not completely democratic. It is also a **capitalist** country with great class privileges and (even now, after a war that has tended to equalise everybody) with great differences in wealth. But nevertheless it is a country in which people have lived together for several hundred years without major conflict, in which the laws are relatively just and official news and statistics can almost invariably be believed, and, last but not least, in which to hold and to voice minority views does not involve any mortal danger.

Key quotations

The pigs did not actually work, but directed and supervised the others. With their superior knowledge it was natural that they should assume the leadership. *(Chapter III)*

Activity 4

1. Find longer definitions of 'fascism', 'communism', 'capitalism' and 'socialism'. Then use an online search engine to find examples of each of them in action.

2. Discuss how each of these ideologies is reflected in the novel. What do you think Orwell wanted to show about each one?

3. Discuss what each of these systems means for ordinary working people. Is it possible for any of them to work for the benefit of everyone in society? Debate your thoughts with others in the class.

Changing attitudes to *Animal Farm*

Orwell was doubtful about *Animal Farm*'s publication at all while Britain was still allied with the Soviet Union. One publisher told him:

> The **fable** does follow, as I see now, so completely the progress of the Russian Soviets and their two dictators that it can apply only to Russia, to the exclusion of other dictatorships. Another thing: it would be less offensive if the predominant caste in the fable were not pigs.

capitalism a political system where everything is owned by individuals or corporations working to make a profit

fable a story with a moral in which animals are the main characters

An article by Steve Pyle in 'The Antigonish Review 111', a Canadian online literary magazine, sums up contemporary views of the book.

> Considering Orwell's obsession with prosaic precision and his hallmark style of plain, straight forward English, it's a wonder how misrepresented and misunderstood the little book became. Orwell's primary theme, of course, was condemnation of tyranny. Yet beyond that, some Socialists saw a message that the Russian revolution could have been successful if not for betrayal. Others... said Russian-style revolution was doomed to failure because its violence gave licence to violence afterwards, in the name of preserving the new status quo. In some quarters, especially in the United States, the book was heralded as proof that Socialism could never work. To the consternation of Orwell it was used as anti-Communist propaganda.

Those who read the book soon after it was published, up until the 1980s, would have done so against the background of the **Cold War** and the **Iron Curtain**. This meant that few people had any first-hand knowledge of what was going on in the Soviet Union, beyond the propaganda fed to the media by both sides. The threat of a third world war seemed all too real, as both the USSR and the USA developed more and more effective nuclear weapons. Only the reality of MAD (Mutual Assured Destruction) appeared to be preventing their use, and civilian populations were issued with instructions about what to do in the event of the **four-minute warning**. It seemed as though the world was divided into two spheres – capitalism and communism.

US President Kennedy peers over the Berlin Wall, one of the strongest symbols of the division of East and West during the Cold War

Cold War a phrase invented by Orwell to describe the state of military and political stand-off that existed between West and East. There were threats and tensions, but neither side could risk another real war

four-minute warning the amount of time that would elapse between a nuclear missile being launched and its arrival at its target

Iron Curtain a metaphor used by Winston Churchill among others to describe the border defences that separated East and West in Europe

When the animated film of the book was made in 1954, the ending of the story was changed so that the animals finally gathered together to stage a revolution against the pigs and take control of the farm. The book's final meeting between pigs and men, showing the two groups becoming identical, was removed, so that capitalism (humans) was separated from **totalitarian** communism (pigs). This fitted with Cold War views of western capitalism and eastern communism.

Modern readers of the book are more likely to see it as a warning against tyranny in general and the corruption caused by power. Orwell himself said:

> Of course I intended it primarily as a **satire** on the Russian revolution. But I did mean it to have a wider application in so much as I meant that that kind of revolution (violent conspiratorial revolution, led by unconsciously power-hungry people) can only lead to a change of masters. I meant the moral to be that revolutions only effect a radical improvement when the masses are alert and know how to chuck out their leaders as soon as the latter have done their job. The turning point of the story was supposed to be when the pigs kept the milk and apples for themselves... If the other animals had had the sense to put their foot down, it would have been all right.

In his article 'Animal Farm: Sixty Years On', Robert Pearce commented:

> No doubt Orwell could have written an unambiguous propagandist pamphlet. Yet we should be grateful that instead he wrote a work of art, something which by its very nature is open to divergent interpretations. Animal Farm is a superb but ambiguous satire on a particular revolution. It is also a more general **allegory**, into which human imagination will continue to breathe life in unexpected ways.

allegory an extended comparison in which events and characters represent other things

satire a form of expression or literary work in which vices, follies, abuses and shortcomings are exaggerated or held up to ridicule, with the intention of reforming the person or society being mocked

totalitarian a situation where the state holds total control over its citizens

Activity 5

As a political novel, *Animal Farm* has been open to different interpretations, often according to the political beliefs of the reader. Working with a partner, imagine you have been asked to contribute a five-minute slot to a radio programme about Orwell. You are going to cover the ways in which readers' attitudes to *Animal Farm* have changed over time, using the information in this chapter. You should include the following:

- attitudes when the book was first written and the Soviet Union was still an ally of Britain and the USA

- attitudes during the Cold War when Europe was divided into East and West

- attitudes of modern readers since the break-up of the USSR and the collapse of communism

- references to *Animal Farm* to illustrate your points

- your own views about what the book represents for you.

You could also find some suitable music to introduce your segment of the programme.

Writing about context

This context section is to help you understand the book and George Orwell's reasons for writing it.

It is important to remember that you should only include contextual information in your assessment response if that is one of the assessment objectives for your exam board. If that is the case, then you should relate the text to Orwell's presentation of English society and culture, as well as his critique of Stalinist communism. For example, the way in which humans (the rich) exploit and oppress the animals (the working class) was made clear by the events in the Soviet Union.

Otherwise you do not need to include contextual information, except to show that you have understood the author's intentions. Writing in depth about how the executed workers resemble the dissident members of the party who were purged, for example, will not gain you any marks. Including a brief reference to the fact that Orwell was writing a satire about Stalinist communism may get recognition.

The humans

Mr Jones

Jones is the owner of Manor Farm. He drinks too much and mistreats the animals: 'Mr Jones, of the Manor Farm, had locked the hen-houses for the night, but was too drunk to remember to shut the pop-holes.' *(Chapter I)* His only answer when the starving animals try to get their own food is to set about them with whips. The rebellion happens when they turn on him and the humans are too surprised to stop themselves being driven from the farm.

Mr Jones looks like evil personified in the 1954 film of *Animal Farm*

Jones is the counterpart of Tsar Nicholas II, who ruled over a backward country and ordered the military to shoot the workers when they went on strike. Instead, the soldiers joined the workers and the Russian revolution took place.

Jones's role in the novel is to show the evils of capitalism as he represents private ownership of property and animals. His fate also parallels the fate of the Tsar. Later Jones is used by the pigs as a threat to keep the other animals obedient. Squealer's constant question is "surely there is no one among you who wants to see Jones come back?" *(Chapter III)*

> **Key quotations**
>
> In past years Mr Jones, although a hard master, had been a capable farmer, but of late he had fallen on evil days. [...] His men were idle and dishonest, the fields were full of weeds, the buildings wanted roofing, the hedges were neglected and the animals were underfed. *(Chapter II)*

Mr Frederick

Frederick is the owner of neighbouring Pinchfield Farm and is described as 'a tough, shrewd man, perpetually involved in lawsuits and with a name for driving hard bargains' *(Chapter IV)*. He is an enemy to Pilkington, who owns the farm on the other side of Manor Farm. Napoleon plays them off against each other, treating Frederick alternately as a friend or enemy and trying to force up the price of timber he wishes to sell. Napoleon thinks that he has outwitted Frederick by insisting on banknotes instead of a cheque, but these are forged and Frederick has the last laugh.

Frederick represents Adolf Hitler who made a non-aggression pact with Stalin, but later invaded Russia anyway. This resulted in the Battle for Moscow in which many Russians were killed. In the novel, this equates to the Battle of the Windmill. 'They had won, but they were weary and bleeding. [...] The sight of their dead comrades stretched upon the grass moved some of them to tears.' *(Chapter VIII)*

Frederick's role in the novel is to show the evils of fascism and to remind readers that some humans are as strong and ruthless as the pigs. He nearly succeeds in taking over

Animal Farm and manages to wreck the windmill completely, as well as defrauding Napoleon over his trade agreement.

Mr Pilkington

Mr Pilkington owns Foxwood, a neighbouring farm to Manor Farm. He is always arguing with Mr Frederick. He is presented as 'an easy-going gentleman-farmer who spent most of his time in fishing or hunting according to the season' (Chapter IV). He takes no part in invading Animal Farm or destroying the windmill.

Later in the book, Napoleon buys land from Pilkington and even invites him to dinner, along with other local farmers. Pilkington toasts Animal Farm and 'once again congratulated the pigs on the low rations, the long working-hours and the general absence of pampering which he had observed on Animal Farm' (Chapter X).

Pilkington represents the British and American leaders who were allies of Stalin in the Second World War, although the row that breaks out at the end of the book may foreshadow the Cold War. He also represents the upper classes both in his 'hunting, shooting and fishing' pursuits and in his attitude to the working class, shown by his 'joke' at the pigs' dinner party: '"If you have your lower animals to contend with," he said, "we have our lower classes!"'(Chapter X)

Pilkington's role in the story is to act as a contrasting character to Frederick and provide an alternative ally for Napoleon.

Activity 1

1. Work in a group of three, with each person taking Jones, Pilkington or Frederick as their subject. Search the text for references to your character and make a note of the pages.

2. Discuss and make a list of similarities and differences between the three men. What do you think Orwell was trying to say about the ruling class in general? Why do you think there was no rebellion at Foxwood or Pinchfield after Animal Farm was established?

3. Look at the quotations below about other humans in the novel. What impression of humans do you think Orwell is trying to give the reader? Write your answer on a slip of paper, giving your reasons. Put your slip into a box with everyone else's and draw them at random in order to create a class discussion.

A fat red-faced man in check breeches and gaiters, who looked like a publican, was stroking her nose and feeding her with sugar. (Chapter V)

... the sight of Napoleon, on all fours, delivering orders to Whymper, who stood on two legs, roused their pride and partly reconciled them to the new arrangement. (Chapter VI)

"Alfred Simmonds, Horse Slaughterer and Glue Boiler, Willingdon. Dealer in Hides and Bone-Meal. Kennels Supplied." (Chapter IX)

The men employed by Jones are shown to be 'idle and dishonest' (Chapter II)

Mr Whymper

Whymper is a go-between for Animal Farm and humans elsewhere. Napoleon also uses him for outside propaganda purposes; Napoleon deliberately walks him past overflowing bins so that Whymper will believe that all is well on the farm and tell others when, in fact, the animals are close to starvation.

Whymper stands for the intellectuals in the West, who were deceived into thinking that Stalin and the Soviet Union had a well-managed economy and happy, prosperous workers. His role in the novel is to act as a bridge between the earlier days of Napoleon's rule and his final conversion into a dictator-like oppressor.

> **Activity 2**
>
> Discuss what Whymper's arrival on the farm might mean after all the animals' efforts to get rid of their human masters.

> **Key quotations**
>
> He was a sly-looking little man with side whiskers, a solicitor in a very small way of business, but sharp enough to have realised earlier than anyone else that Animal Farm would need a broker and that the commissions would be worth having. *(Chapter VI)*

The animals

Old Major

Old Major is the senior animal on the farm, who is responsible for laying down the principles of Animalism and making the case for the Rebellion. He is an inspiring speaker and leader, and teaches the animals their rousing anthem, 'Beasts of England'. 'Old Major (so he was always called, though the name under which he had been exhibited was Willingdon Beauty) was so highly regarded on the farm that everyone was quite ready to lose an hour's sleep in order to hear what he had to say.' *(Chapter I)*

He represents Karl Marx (the founder of Marxism) and also has elements of Lenin. Like Marx, he dies before he can see his philosophy translated into action and, like Lenin, he never sees the corruption of his ideals by those who seize power for themselves. He can be criticized for having **authoritarian** views as his system relies on everyone having the same ideas and goals.

His role in the novel is to show the animals, and thus the readers, the possibilities of a political system founded on justice and equality for all.

authoritarian favouring obedience to authority over personal freedom

> **Key quotations**
>
> "All the habits of Man are evil. And above all, no animal must ever tyrannise over his own kind. Weak or strong, clever or simple, we are all brothers. No animal must ever kill any other animal. All animals are equal." *(Chapter I)*

Napoleon

Napoleon is named after the military leader who won favour with republican France and then proclaimed himself emperor. He is the villain in the story who uses the Rebellion to his own advantage. 'Napoleon was a large, rather fierce-looking Berkshire boar, the only Berkshire on the farm, not much of a talker but with a reputation for getting his own way.' *(Chapter II)*

Napoleon and Snowball are the leaders of the Rebellion, teaching the other animals about Animalism and trying to educate them. However, once the Rebellion is complete, Napoleon begins to plan a takeover of the farm, using Squealer to subvert the message of Animalism and using the dogs to enforce his decisions. He has public disagreements with Snowball and eventually uses the dogs to drive him out.

Napoleon makes use of propaganda by using the pigeons, and later Whymper, to spread news of the Rebellion's success to other farms. He also uses propaganda, misinformation and the rewriting of history to persuade the animals that Snowball is a traitor and that he, Napoleon, is a hero. For example, he sends Squealer to say that "Snowball was in league with Jones from the very start! He was Jones's secret agent all the time. It has all been proved by documents which he left behind him and which we have only just discovered." *(Chapter VII)* Anyone who disagrees with him is made to confess to being in league with Snowball and is then executed by the dogs.

It soon becomes clear that Napoleon has little interest in equality or improving the lives of the animals. Instead he keeps the support of most of the pigs and the dogs by giving them preferential treatment and relies on the lies told by Squealer, fear of the dogs and the relative stupidity of the other animals to gain more and more control. By the end of the book, he has betrayed every aspect of Animalism and the Rebellion, not to mention his fellow animals.

Activity 3

Discuss how Orwell presents points of similarity between Napoleon and Jones at various stages of the novel. You should consider such things as:

- the way they assume control
- their abuse of alcohol and fine living
- the way they merge together at the end of the novel.
- the way they treat the other animals
- their reactions to Moses the raven

Napoleon makes himself into a cult figure, even awarding himself medals to reinforce his image as a hero (in the 1954 film)

Napoleon stands for Joseph Stalin, one of the worst dictators of the 20th century, who took advantage of the Russian revolution after Lenin's death to take power and repress any opposition.

Napoleon's role in the book is to show how a ruthless leader can use a popular uprising to seize power for themselves. He also shows how much a dictator can get away with, as the majority of the animals put up with being exploited and starved.

Key quotations

Napoleon was now never spoken of simply as "Napoleon". He was always referred to in formal style as "our Leader, Comrade Napoleon", and the pigs liked to invent for him such titles as Father of All Animals, Terror of Mankind, Protector of the Sheepfold, Ducklings' Friend, and the like. *(Chapter VIII)*

Activity 4

Working in a group of five, take two chapters of the book each. Each person should select the following from their chapters:

a) what Napoleon says – a summary of his speech with some short quotations

b) what Napoleon does – a summary of his actions with some short quotations

c) what the narrator tells us about Napoleon – with some short quotations

d) how the other characters react to Napoleon – with some short quotations.

Present your findings as a timeline, showing what you have learned about Napoleon at each stage and supporting your ideas with references and quotations.

Snowball

Snowball is one of the original leaders that emerged, along with Napoleon, while the animals were preparing for the Rebellion: **'Snowball was a more vivacious pig than Napoleon, quicker in speech and more inventive, but was not considered to have the same depth of character.'** *(Chapter II)* He is the one who designs the flag and explains its meaning to the animals. He tries hard to organize the animals into committees, which are failures, but also tries to educate them, with some degree of success. However, he also reduces the commandments to the meaningless slogan **"Four legs good, two legs bad"** *(Chapter III)*.

Snowball is proven to be the best military leader in the Battle of the Cowshed. Snowball and Napoleon lead the weekly debates but they disagree about everything. The most important quarrel is over the windmill, which leads to Snowball's expulsion.

Snowball is innovative and seems to genuinely care for the welfare of the animals. He seeks approval for his ideas through the democratic process of meetings and debates, although few of the animals have the intelligence to engage in this. However, he also goes along with the appropriation of the milk and apples for the pigs and he doesn't consider how the animals will pay for the machinery needed to run the windmill.

Snowball is clever and plans the design of the windmill

Snowball is the counterpart of Leon Trotsky, the head of the Soviet army, who had many ideas for making communism work at home and abroad. He was exiled and later killed by Stalin.

Snowball's role in the novel is to show an alternative form of leadership to Napoleon's. Napoleon demonizes Snowball after his absence by blaming him for everything that goes wrong, as well as rewriting history to show him as a traitor to the animals and in league with the humans. Snowball becomes the scapegoat for all the things that go wrong on the farm and is turned into a worse threat than Jones: **'Whenever anything went wrong it became usual to attribute it to Snowball.'** *(Chapter VII)* Napoleon takes all the credit for Snowball's achievements, while lying to such an extent that even Boxer is doubtful of Squealer's explanations. The last thing we hear about Snowball is that he's been forgotten.

Key quotations

The animals were thoroughly frightened. It seemed to them as though Snowball were some kind of invisible influence, pervading the air about them and menacing them with all kinds of dangers. *(Chapter VII)*

Tips for assessment

Exam questions may ask you to write about the role or function of a character, their importance to the novel or how Orwell presents them. Remember to focus your answer clearly on whichever aspect you have been asked about.

Squealer

As his name implies, Squealer is Napoleon's chief spy and informant, who acts as his mouthpiece to the other animals and reports back on any grumbling or dissension. He is described as 'a small fat pig named Squealer, with very round cheeks, twinkling eyes, nimble movements and a shrill voice. He was a brilliant talker [...] The others said of Squealer that he could turn black into white.' (Chapter II) It is this skill that Napoleon finds most useful when he wants the animals to believe that everything he does is for their benefit.

In the beginning, Squealer works with Napoleon and Snowball to teach the animals about Animalism. Soon he is justifying the theft of the milk and apples on the grounds that the pigs need them for their health and that, without the pigs' vigilance, Jones would come back – an argument he uses to silence any opposition.

His appearance of being merry and persuasive is undermined by Orwell in occasional phrases that suggest an underlying malice, such as 'he cast a very ugly look at Boxer with his little twinkling eyes' (Chapter VII) and 'his little eyes darted suspicious glances from side to side' (Chapter IX). He is the most powerful creature on the farm after Napoleon.

Squealer relies on the animals not trusting their own memories or thoughts sufficiently to argue with him. Since most of them cannot read or write, they are unable to refute his version of events. When the animals are surprised at Napoleon's decision to build the windmill, Squealer convinces them it is Napoleon's cunning: 'This, said Squealer, was something called tactics. He repeated a number of times, "Tactics, comrades, tactics!" skipping round and whisking his tail with a merry laugh. The animals were not certain what the word meant, but Squealer spoke so persuasively, and the three dogs who happened to be with him growled so threateningly, that they accepted his explanation without further questions.' *(Chapter V)* He uses a mixture of persuasion and threat to crush any doubts.

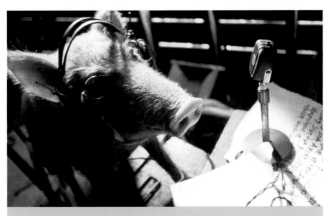

Squealer, in the 1999 film, uses his skill with words to deceive the hard-working animals

Squealer is the most interesting of the pigs in terms of dialogue. At the beginning, we are told he can make black into white and throughout the story Orwell shows this ability in action. When the animals recall a prohibition about trading with humans, Squealer asks, **"Are you certain that this is not something that you have dreamed, comrades? Have you any record of such a resolution? Is it written down anywhere?"** *(Chapter VI)* It is noticeable that to Squealer, unlike old Major, a dream is not something to be followed. If all else fails, he merely asks the animals if they want Jones to come back, a simple ploy which makes Jones into a monster in their imagination.

He is nowhere to be seen at the Battle of the Windmill, but the alteration of the Seven Commandments is explained (at least to the reader) when he is found around midnight at the bottom of a broken ladder near a lantern and a pot of paint.

Squealer seems to represent the Soviet newspaper *Pravda*, which was the only way the Russian people could receive news, much of which was written by Stalin.

Key quotations

There was nothing with which they could compare their present lives: they had nothing to go upon except Squealer's lists of figures, which invariably demonstrated that everything was getting better and better. *(Chapter X)*

Activity 6

1. Look through the book and make a note of all Squealer's exchanges with the animals. Then sort through these exchanges in chronological order, highlighting all the stages by which old Major's precepts are abandoned. Discuss and note the arguments used by Squealer each time to justify these changes.

2. Using the list of rhetorical devices in Activity 1 of the 'Plot and Structure' section (page 7), contrast one of Squealer's speeches with that of old Major's speech at the start of the book. What similarities and differences do you notice in their styles and what does this suggest about the way that Animalism has been corrupted?

Boxer

Boxer is the largest and strongest animal on the farm and much of the work depends on him: 'he was universally respected for his steadiness of character and tremendous powers of work.' *(Chapter I)*

He is one of the most dedicated workers for the Rebellion. He and Clover explain the principles of Animalism to the other animals. Boxer even burns the straw hat that keeps the flies off his ears when he hears that animals should be naked. He is not clever, though, and only manages to learn the first four letters of the alphabet.

> ## Activity 7
>
> 1. Working in groups of four, take two chapters each from Chapter II to Chapter IX. Each person should find one or two quotations from each chapter that show how Orwell presents Boxer in the novel.
>
> 2. On a large sheet of paper, draw a picture of Boxer. Surround it with the quotations from your group. For each quotation, add a comment box that gives your view of what it tells the reader about Boxer.

At the Battle of the Cowshed, for which he is awarded a medal, Boxer terrifies the humans and floors a stable boy. However, he is a kind and gentle beast, and has tears in his eyes when he thinks he has killed the lad. He admires the pigs for their intelligence and decides that **"Napoleon is always right"** *(Chapter V)*, despite his own doubts about the abolition of the debates and the expulsion of Snowball. His solution to unpleasant situations like the mass executions is to work even harder, rather than questioning the leadership. His naivety leads him to believe in Napoleon, but his faith is horribly shattered at the end. It is unfortunate that Boxer adopts this uncritical attitude to Napoleon, because he is the only animal who could have united the rest against him and the only one strong enough to deal with the dogs.

When Boxer is too ill and weak to work, he is repaid with callous cruelty by Napoleon (in the 1954 film)

Boxer represents the proletariat, or working classes, of the Soviet Union. Stalin relied on their labour and their obedience to implement his reforms.

Boxer's role in the book is to show the gullibility of the animals, who do what the pigs tell them and cannot think or act for themselves. His two slogans are **"I will work harder"** *(Chapter V)* and **"Napoleon is always right"** *(Chapter V)*. Even when he is attacked by the dogs, he looks to Napoleon for guidance about what to do. He provides a dreadful example of what the animals can expect when they have outlived their usefulness.

> **Key quotations**
>
> **Boxer was the admiration of everybody. He had been a hard worker even in Jones's time, but now he seemed more like three horses than one; there were days when the entire work of the farm seemed to rest upon his mighty shoulders. [...] His answer to every problem, every setback, was "I will work harder!"** – which he had adopted as his personal motto.** *(Chapter III)*

Tips for assessment

In an extract-based question about a character, remember to focus on the details of the extract itself. Only mention other incidents elsewhere in the book if they add insight to a point you are making or if you are asked to relate the extract to the rest of the book.

Clover

Clover is also a carthorse. She is described as 'a stout motherly mare approaching middle life' *(Chapter I)*. She is a mother to all the animals, as well as an uncomplaining worker. Her first act in the story is to provide a safe haven for a crowd of lost ducklings.

Although a bit cleverer than Boxer, Clover is unable to read and absorbs the pigs' teachings equally without question. It is she who quietly reprimands Mollie for talking to humans and tries to persuade her to adopt Animalism.

Clover tries to make Boxer look after his health. She treats Boxer's injuries after the Battle of the Windmill and urges him to work less hard. When he collapses, it is Clover who sends for help and when Benjamin reads the terrible words on the van, she drives herself into a canter to try to save Boxer.

Instead of taking Squealer's assurances at face value, she does make some attempt to verify them by getting Muriel to read the commandments to her. It is she who sees what a long way the animals have come from the ideals of the Rebellion. She is the first to see the pigs walking on two legs and it is she who leads the way for the animals to see the humans and pigs together at the end of the book.

It is Clover who keeps the memory of the Rebellion alive in her old age and passes on its ideals, as well as 'Beasts of England', to the younger animals. Like Boxer, Clover stands for the proletariat who believed in the communist revolution and fought and worked hard for it, continuing even after it had been hijacked by Stalin and turned into a savage **dictatorship**.

Her role in the novel is to show the changes in the commandments and to voice the bewildered despair of the animals, who see their Rebellion going so horribly wrong. It is also her role to keep the ideals first propounded by old Major alive for future generations in the hope that one day his dream might be realized.

dictatorship government by a single leader with total power

Key quotations

Whatever happened she would remain faithful, work hard, carry out the orders that were given to her, and accept the leadership of Napoleon. But still, it was not for this that she and all the other animals had hoped and toiled. It was not for this that they had built the windmill and faced the pellets of Jones's gun. Such were her thoughts, though she lacked the words to express them. *(Chapter VII)*

Activity 8

Clover is one of the few animals to survive to the end of the novel. With a partner, discuss:

a) Why do you think Orwell might have chosen her to be one who survives?

b) Why is she the first to see the pigs walking on two legs?

c) Why is it Clover who leads the animals to see that the pigs and humans have become the same?

Exchange ideas with others in the class.

Benjamin

Benjamin is a donkey and Orwell gives him the morose character that many literary donkeys have.

Key quotations

Benjamin was the oldest animal on the farm, and the worst tempered. He seldom talked, and when he did it was usually to make some cynical remark [...] Nevertheless, without openly admitting it, he was devoted to Boxer [...] *(Chapter I)*

He is completely cynical and will not believe that any political or social system will improve the lives of the animals for long. Although he can read well, he refuses to do so most of the time. The only times he breaks this rule is when he reads out what is on the van that takes Boxer away and when he tells Clover how the commandments have been altered finally to a single one. Although he has no enthusiasm for Animalism, he continues to work in the way he has always done and he plays his part in the Battle of the Cowshed, using his small hooves. He doesn't take sides during the argument over the windmill, as he thinks that whatever happens life will go on badly as before.

However, he works on the windmill, pulling a small cart with Muriel, the goat. He also joins Clover and the others in their sad huddle after the executions. It is Benjamin who realizes that Frederick and his men are using explosives to blow up the windmill and he warns the other animals. He is also the only one who knows what Squealer has been up to when he is found with the paint pot by the ladder.

Benjamin joins Clover in trying to persuade Boxer to save his health and strength and, when his friend collapses, he lies beside him to whisk the flies off Boxer with his tail. The only time he shows any excitement or moves fast is when the van arrives to take Boxer away. He warns the animals what the van says and where Boxer is being taken, although too late for him to be saved. After Boxer's death he becomes even more taciturn than before.

Benjamin has his own morose way of speaking that reflects his nature. '**When asked whether he was not happier now that Jones was gone, he would say only "Donkeys live a long time. None of you has ever seen a dead donkey," and the others had to be content with this cryptic answer.**' *(Chapter III)* It seems to mean that he has seen regimes come and go, and none of them were any different in the end.

Activity 9

1. Why does Orwell show Benjamin as one of the few survivors, along with Clover, at the end of the novel?

2. Why does Orwell show him as cynical and pessimistic? Do you think Benjamin is proved right at the end of the novel?

3. In your opinion, why does Orwell give him this cryptic way of speaking, which puzzles the other animals? What kind of character is he presenting?

Benjamin represents those members of the Soviet Union who expected little benefit from the revolution or from their leaders.

His role in the novel is to show that the **idealists** are bound to be disappointed by the corruption of power. He doesn't really believe that the Rebellion will solve anything and he knows that there will always be a gap between those who have power and those who don't.

idealist someone who is influenced by ideals rather than practical considerations

Old Benjamin, the donkey, seemed quite unchanged since the Rebellion. He did his work in the same slow obstinate way as he had done it in Jones's time, never shirking and never volunteering for extra work either. About the Rebellion and its results he would express no opinion. *(Chapter III)*

Activity 10

Work in a group of three. Imagine that Boxer, Clover and Benjamin decided to stand up to the pigs and persuade the other animals to join them. What qualities would each of them bring to such a **coalition**?

Discuss how they might go about creating their own rebellion. Use your ideas to write an extra scene for the story, before Boxer's collapse, where you show these three trying to persuade the other animals to rise up against Napoleon.

You could write this as an extra short chapter, or as a play scene, if you prefer.

Remember to stay true to the animals' characters as they are portrayed by Orwell, but with a new sense of mission. Decide which of the animals join them and why.

coalition an agreement between different groups to work together in a common interest

Muriel

Muriel is the only goat on the farm. 'Muriel, the goat, could read somewhat better than the dogs, and sometimes used to read to the others in the evenings from scraps of newspaper which she found on the rubbish heap.' *(Chapter III)* Her ability to read makes her useful to Clover when she needs reminding of the commandments. She is quite close to Clover and is also a hard worker and faithful supporter of the Rebellion, although she questions Squealer about the banning of 'Beasts of England'.

Muriel represents the educated workers who could think for themselves but who lacked the personality or leadership to encourage others to stand against the rulers.

Her role in the story is to show how the pigs alter the principles of Animalism to suit their own arrogance and greed.

But a few days later Muriel, reading over the Seven Commandments to herself, noticed that there was yet another of them which the animals had remembered wrong. They had thought the Fifth Commandment was "No animal shall drink alcohol", but there were two words that they had forgotten. Actually the Commandment read: "No animal shall drink alcohol *to excess*." *(Chapter VIII)*

Mollie

Mollie is an attractive horse and extremely vain: 'At the last moment Mollie, the foolish, pretty white mare who drew Mr Jones's trap, came mincing daintily in, chewing at a lump of sugar. She took a place near the front and began flirting her white mane, hoping to draw attention to the red ribbons it was plaited with.' *(Chapter I)* This vanity is a sign of her self-interest.

She doesn't like the idea of giving up sugar and ribbons and being expected to work alongside the other animals. She seldom did her share of the work, refused to learn to read anything other than her name, which she made into an attractive display.

Clover catches Mollie fraternizing with the humans of Foxwood, who feed her sugar, and she finds a pile of ribbons in her stall. Eventually Mollie disappears and is spotted later by the pigeons, having sold out to the human enemy. She is seen as a traitor and wiped from the animals' memories.

Mollie stands for those who did not want revolution in Russia because it made them worse off. Many of them left for Western Europe or elsewhere and made new lives.

Her role in the novel is to show that not all the animals are in agreement over the changes to the farm. In the light of what happens later, some might consider that Mollie makes the wisest choice, even if for the wrong reasons.

> **Key quotations**
>
> Three days later Mollie disappeared. For some weeks nothing was known of her whereabouts, then the pigeons reported that they had seen her on the other side of Willingdon. [...] A fat red-faced man in check breeches and gaiters, who looked like a publican, was stroking her nose and feeding her with sugar. [...] None of the animals ever mentioned Mollie again. *(Chapter V)*

Moses

Moses is described as 'the tame raven, who slept on a perch behind the back door' *(Chapter I)*. He is Jones's informant. He is also a persuasive speaker and promises the animals a paradise after death called Sugarcandy Mountain. He is given the name of the famous Israelite leader in the Old Testament who led his people to 'the Promised Land'.

We are told that he is not at the meeting addressed by old Major. When the Rebellion occurs, Moses follows Mrs Jones when she flees from the farm.

When Moses returns to the farm, years later, it is after Napoleon has become total dictator. The pigs allow him to stay and give him beer, as Jones used to do. The raven continues to talk to the animals about Sugarcandy Mountain. In former days, some of the animals believed his stories. When he returns, their lives are even harder under Napoleon and so more animals want to believe his stories.

Moses represents religious leaders who tried to reconcile the poor to their hard lives by claiming they would get their reward in the afterlife. Marx discouraged religion because he felt it prevented people from finding their own solutions to their misery. Marx felt that leaders encouraged it, because they hoped it would prevent the workers from rising against them.

Moses' role in the book is to show the hypocrisy both of Jones and of Napoleon, who encourages Moses to make his false promises, while employing him as a spy. He also reveals the naivety of many of the animals who believe his stories.

> **Key quotations**
>
> "Up there, comrades," he would say solemnly, pointing to the sky with his large beak – "up there, just on the other side of that dark cloud that you can see – there it lies, Sugarcandy Mountain, that happy country where we poor animals shall rest for ever from our labours." *(Chapter IX)*

The cat

Like most of her kind, the cat is an independent creature who purrs 'contentedly throughout Major's speech without listening to a word of what he was saying' *(Chapter I)*. She has no political views. She is not given a name, unlike the other animals, which makes her more mysterious.

The cat doesn't join in the general work of the farm, but occasionally she helps out, as in the Battle of the Cowshed. Her guiding principle seems to be self-interest, but, unlike Mollie, she has no wish to take orders from either humans or pigs.

The cat seems to stand for those in society who are apolitical and do not become involved with workers or rulers. The role of the cat is to show the possibility of being on neither side while keeping in with everyone.

> **Activity 11**
>
> Mollie, Moses and the cat all find different solutions to their lack of enthusiasm for the new regime at Animal Farm.
>
> Imagine you are a reporter for a local newspaper who has managed to track down these three characters and interview them. Write an article of around 200–300 words with the heading 'Animal Dissenters' in which you report your interviews. Keep as close as you can to the book itself and use what you have read to imagine what these three might say to show themselves in the best light.

The dogs

Apart from the parents, the dogs are not named. Reared by Napoleon in seclusion, they become fierce and loyal bodyguards who obey his orders. 'Though not yet full-grown they were huge dogs, and as fierce-looking as wolves. They kept close to Napoleon. It was noticed that they wagged their tails to him in the same way as the other dogs had been used to do to Mr Jones.' *(Chapter V)* Their

The use of deadly dogs is the sign of an oppressive dictator, not a benevolent leader

obedience to Napoleon foreshadows the way in which Napoleon and the pigs turn into humans at the end of the novel.

The other animals are terrified of the dogs, with good reason, since they are also Napoleon's executioners. Their menacing growls are enough to silence any opposition. Unlike the other animals, they never speak.

The dogs are the counterparts of the KGB, Stalin's feared secret police, who killed and tortured millions of Soviet citizens. Their role in the story is to show how Napoleon gained, and kept, power through violence and intimidation.

Key quotations

When they had finished their confession the dogs promptly tore their throats out, and in a terrible voice Napoleon demanded whether any other animal had anything to confess. *(Chapter VII)*

The hens

Although they are described as some of the stupider animals by Orwell, the hens are the only animals to attempt a rebellion against Napoleon in an effort to save their eggs. It does not help them for several die and their leaders are later executed. Their role in the novel is to show what happens to those who oppose Napoleon without the strength to defeat the dogs.

The sheep

These are the unthinking animals that are too stupid even to remember the commandments. They can only learn a simple slogan after much repetition and then they bleat it in unison for minutes at a time. Napoleon uses them to silence opposition as they drown out other speakers. Quite unable to think for themselves, they simply follow orders from those in power.

Key quotations

When they had once got it by heart the sheep developed a great liking for this maxim, and often as they lay in the field they would all start bleating "Four legs good, two legs bad! Four legs good, two legs bad!" and keep it up for hours on end, never growing tired of it. *(Chapter III)*

The pigeons

They are used by Napoleon to spread messages and propaganda to neighbouring farms. At first they tell other animals about the Rebellion, which creates disturbances on local farms. Later they are used to send messages between Napoleon and Pilkington. They also give early warning of any invasion of Animal Farm from outside.

Key quotations

Every day Snowball and Napoleon sent out flights of pigeons whose instructions were to mingle with the animals on neighbouring farms, tell them the story of the Rebellion, and teach them the tune of 'Beasts of England'. *(Chapter IV)*

Activity 12

Consider the following questions.

a) In what ways does Orwell use the stereotypes of the animals (e.g. the sheep) for his own purposes in the book? How far does he give them personalities of their own?

b) What effect does this have on the events in the book?

Make a large spider diagram to show your thoughts and ideas. You should include references and quotations to support them.

Writing about characters

Upgrade

You may be asked to answer a question about a character, or sometimes a group of characters, from the novel. You will need to show your knowledge and understanding of them not just as a person/animal, but as a created character. You will need to cover the following in your answer:

• the kind of things the author gives the character to say and how they say them

• the kind of things the author gives the character to do and how they do them

• what the author makes the narrator tell us about the character

• how the author makes other characters react to them

• why the author has included this character in the novel (their role or function).

You will need to give detailed evidence from the novel to support all the points you make, including quotations where appropriate.

Character map

Idealistic leaders

Common animals

Napoleon's elite

Human sympathizers

Independent thinkers

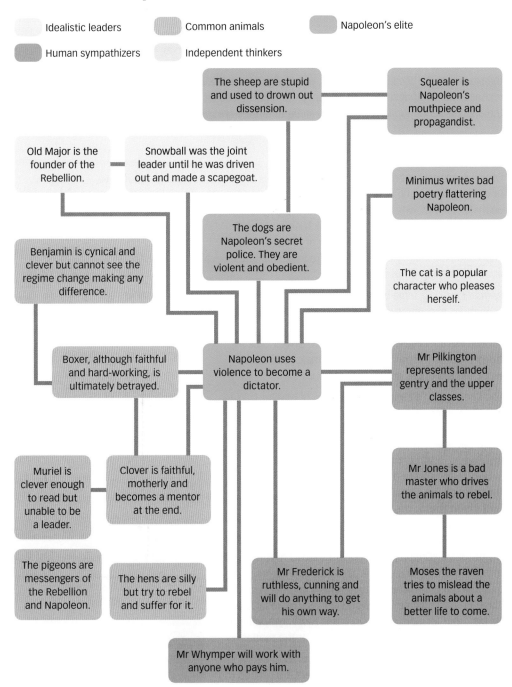

The sheep are stupid and used to drown out dissension.

Squealer is Napoleon's mouthpiece and propagandist.

Old Major is the founder of the Rebellion.

Snowball was the joint leader until he was driven out and made a scapegoat.

Minimus writes bad poetry flattering Napoleon.

Benjamin is cynical and clever but cannot see the regime change making any difference.

The dogs are Napoleon's secret police. They are violent and obedient.

The cat is a popular character who pleases herself.

Boxer, although faithful and hard-working, is ultimately betrayed.

Napoleon uses violence to become a dictator.

Mr Pilkington represents landed gentry and the upper classes.

Muriel is clever enough to read but unable to be a leader.

Clover is faithful, motherly and becomes a mentor at the end.

Mr Jones is a bad master who drives the animals to rebel.

The pigeons are messengers of the Rebellion and Napoleon.

The hens are silly but try to rebel and suffer for it.

Mr Frederick is ruthless, cunning and will do anything to get his own way.

Moses the raven tries to mislead the animals about a better life to come.

Mr Whymper will work with anyone who pays him.

Orwell's publisher described the book as a 'prose poem' because of its beautiful writing. Orwell himself was disappointed that his reviewers had not seen the beauty of the book, preferring to concentrate on its political satire. He wrote that it was the first book in which 'I tried with full consciousness of what I was doing to fuse political purpose and artistic purpose into one whole'. It certainly creates a very real world for the reader, partly because of Orwell's knowledge of animals and farming – note the technical details that show his familiarity – and partly because he succeeds in making the animals seem human while at the same time they are recognizably animals.

Allegory

Orwell subtitled his book 'A Fairy Tale'. Fairy tales are fantastical stories that have underlying truths and warnings. *Animal Farm* is clearly a fantasy involving talking animals and pigs who learn to read and write, but fairy tales always have happy endings, which *Animal Farm* does not. Orwell is reversing the idea of rewarding the good and punishing the bad in order to make a point about political and class power.

Animal Farm is a fable because it uses animals acting as humans in order to point out a **moral**. However, the moral in most fables is the reward of virtue, whereas in *Animal Farm* it is vice that is rewarded. Orwell is using **irony** here, as the morality of the animals is punished while the evil-doing of the pigs is rewarded.

The book is also a satire on the nature of totalitarian rule. By turning Stalin and his acolytes into pigs, Orwell is making a point about Soviet communism, while the gullibility and apathy of the other animals is a demonstration of the need for working-class people to be alert to the behaviour of the ruling class: 'In spite of the shock that Snowball's expulsion had given them, the animals were dismayed by this announcement. Several of them would have protested if they could have found the right arguments.' *(Chapter V)* Satire is intended to reform through mockery and Orwell uses pigs and humans to make fun of totalitarian government and the ruling class. He also ridicules the working class, represented by the other animals, although this is more sympathetic because he makes their plight moving for the reader.

Most often, *Animal Farm* is referred to as an allegory. This is because the events and characters are related to

In this poster, the 1954 film might be mistaken for a cosy Disney-type movie – but the pig's expression tells another story!

real contemporary happenings and people. Napoleon represents Stalin; Snowball is Trotsky; old Major is Marx, etc. Modern readers might also apply the allegory to other situations where revolutions have led to a new oppression. In addition, the humans become the ruling, or upper class, the pigs represent government by dictators and the other animals are cast as the workers or proletariat: **'There were times when it seemed to the animals that they worked longer hours and fed no better than they had done in Jones's day.'** *(Chapter VIII)*

Activity 1

Find a copy of Plato's 'Allegory of the Cave' and the fable of 'The Tortoise and the Hare'. Read them through and discuss how *Animal Farm* is similar in structure and language. Why do you think Orwell might have chosen to present his ideas in this form? Compare your ideas with others in the class.

Much of *Animal Farm* is written in straightforward prose – Orwell is famous for his journalistic style and lack of **figurative language**. He uses some comparisons, either metaphors or **similes**. The animals describe Squealer being able to **'turn black into white'** *(Chapter II)*, for example, while the dogs are depicted **'as fierce-looking as wolves'** *(Chapter V)*. Orwell uses simple phrases such as **'the work of the farm went like clockwork'** *(Chapter III)* or **'the animals worked like slaves'** *(Chapter VI)* which are **clichés**, but appropriate to the style of a fairy tale. Generally his language is simple and easy to comprehend, which adds to the **mythic** atmosphere of the story.

In the quotation below, there are few words with more than two syllables, e.g. 'years', 'came', 'went', 'short', 'lives', 'fled', 'time', 'by'. This simplicity and transparency of the narration is a useful **foil** to the deviousness of the pigs' propaganda, as well as being suited to the style of a fairy tale.

Key quotations

Years passed. The seasons came and went, the short animal lives fled by. A time came when there was no one who remembered the old days before the Rebellion, except Clover, Benjamin, Moses the raven, and a number of the pigs. *(Chapter X)*

cliché an unoriginal phrase that has been over-used

figurative language language that uses figures of speech, such as comparisons, to take the meaning beyond the literal use of the words, e.g. 'pull your socks up' used figuratively means that you need to make more effort

foil something that acts as an opposite

irony the opposite to what is expected

moral a lesson about life or behaviour

mythic suggesting a myth (a traditional or legendary story)

simile a comparison that uses 'like' or 'as', e.g. 'bright as a button'

Activity 2

Write your own fable. Find a news story and rewrite it in the form of a fable, using animals to point out the moral. Your fable should be no more than 250 words long. You could look at Aesop's fables as exemplars.

Symbolism

Orwell was very conscious of the power of symbols and the way in which they are used by the ruling class. The symbols he uses in *Animal Farm* are related to the symbols used in the Soviet Union, although they are also able to stand on their own. Some of the symbols he uses include:

- The song, 'Beasts of England' (which stands for the 'Internationale'), is one that unites all oppressed animals and spreads widely outside Animal Farm itself. Its replacement by Minimus's lyrics glorifying Napoleon – **"Lord of the swill-bucket"** *(Chapter VIII)* – is never successful.

- The flag, like all flags, is a symbol of the new nation and shows a hoof and horn on a green background, which closely resembles the hammer and sickle on the red of the Soviet flag. The green stands for the fields of Animal Farm, while the hoof and horn represent the supremacy of the animals themselves (as the hammer and sickle represented the Soviet workers).

- When Lenin died, his embalmed body was preserved in a mausoleum. Old Major's skull, which is set up for the animals to file past, is a symbol of the boar himself and a reminder of his dream. Its burial by Napoleon at the end of the novel is a strong statement of the death of the dream.

- The captured gun represents victory, as in all historic battles, and is fired on special occasions, just as the armed forces fire a salute at times like the monarch's birthday.

- The Seven Commandments are a reminder not only of the Ten Commandments of the Old Testament, but of the communist ideals of Marx and Lenin. Their gradual corruption represents the undermining of the principles of equality on which the Rebellion was founded.

- The windmill stands for the aspirations of the animals to modernize and improve the farm and their own lives. Snowball sets out his ideas for how it would work, although without considering how it would be financed. It is destroyed during a storm and has to be rebuilt at enormous cost to the animals (just as the Russian people laboured at their five-year plans). They are enormously proud of their achievement only for it to be blown up by Frederick during the Battle of the Windmill. In the end, it benefits only the pigs, like everything else: **'The windmill, however, had not after all been used for generating electrical power. It was used for milling corn, and brought in a handsome money profit.'** *(Chapter X)*

- The processions that Napoleon uses to establish his own leadership are also ways to impress on the animals that they are part of a great community. They reflect the enormous military parades in Red Square where the Soviet leaders showed off their armaments. The animals are impressed and enjoy the music and processing, if not the speeches: **'But if there were hardships to be borne, they were partly offset by the fact that life nowadays had a greater dignity than it had had before. There were more songs, more speeches, more processions.'** *(Chapter IX)*

During the Cold War, in particular, the Soviet government paraded its most advanced missiles and weaponry to show the West, and the Soviet people, the extent of its great military power

Activity 3

1. Can you find any other ways in which Orwell uses symbols in the story, e.g. the names of the characters? Working with a partner, make a list of further symbols and their meanings as above.

2. Why do you think leaders might make use of symbols, such as flags, mottoes and animals (e.g. the lion or the dragon)?

3. Write two or three paragraphs explaining your ideas about the effect of symbolism on readers of the book.

Irony

The main irony of the story is that a revolution fought in the name of equality becomes a method of perpetuating a different form of tyranny. Orwell was keenly aware of the irony in social and political situations and he includes it in *Animal Farm* in different forms.

Dramatic irony

Throughout the book, the reader is made aware of things the animals don't understand. For example, when the commandments are altered, the reader knows that Squealer is responsible, but the animals think they haven't remembered correctly. This is an example of **dramatic irony**. When Snowball is accused of destroying the windmill, the animals believe it, while the reader is aware that it was due to the storm. After Boxer's death, Napoleon speaks to the animals: 'It had not been possible, he said, to bring back their lamented comrade's remains for interment on the farm, but he had ordered a large wreath to be made from the laurels in the farmhouse garden and sent down to be placed on Boxer's grave.' *(Chapter IX)* The animals believe these lies, but the reader knows that Boxer's body could not be returned because he was slaughtered at the knacker's.

Situational irony

Orwell uses **situational irony** to pinpoint the gradual way in which the equality promised by the Rebellion is undermined. Almost every accusation made against humans by old Major in his rousing speech can be levelled against Napoleon. This extends to the commandments of Animalism devised by the pigs themselves as they prepared for the Rebellion. The irony is that they end up meaning the opposite of what was intended. When the animals first enter the farmhouse, e.g. 'A unanimous resolution was passed on the spot that the farmhouse should be preserved as a museum. All were agreed that no animal must ever live there.' *(Chapter II)* Within a few months the pigs are doing just that and Squealer is justifying it to the animals. Another example of this type of irony is when the dogs return from chasing Snowball and Orwell comments, 'It was noticed that they wagged their tails to him [Napoleon] in the same way as the other dogs had been used to do to Mr Jones.' *(Chapter V)*

Verbal irony

Verbal irony is shown mainly by Squealer in his propaganda speeches to the animals, e.g. when he comments, "No one believes more firmly than Comrade Napoleon that all animals are equal." *(Chapter V)* Since this is when he is explaining the abolition of the weekly debates, the irony is clear. Democracy consists of everyone taking part in the decisions and going with the majority whether the leaders agree with it or not.

Orwell also uses verbal irony in Napoleon's speech when work is announced on Sundays. 'This work was strictly voluntary, but any animal who absented himself from it would have his rations reduced by half.' *(Chapter VI)* It's clear that if sanctions are applied, then the voluntary nature of something is lost. Again, when telling the animals not to expect the windmill to be used for luxuries, 'Napoleon had denounced such ideas as contrary to the spirit of Animalism. The truest happiness, he said, lay in working hard and living frugally.' *(Chapter X)* Unless, of course, you were a pig!

dramatic irony when the reader/audience know something the characters do not (e.g. in *Romeo and Juliet* the audience know Juliet isn't dead, but her family doesn't know)

situational irony when the outcome of an event/action is the reverse of that expected (e.g. being hit by lightning after carefully avoiding trees)

verbal irony when someone says the opposite of what they mean/intend (e.g. 'What a lovely day' when it's pouring with rain)

Activity 4

1. Look at the quotations below and discuss with a partner or in a small group how Orwell is using irony for effect in each case.

> Once again all rations were reduced except those of the pigs and the dogs. *(Chapter IX)*

> About this time, too, it was laid down as a rule that when a pig and any other animal met on the path, the other animal must stand aside *(Chapter IX)*

> Napoleon had commanded that once a week there should be held something called a Spontaneous Demonstration *(Chapter IX)*

> There was only one candidate, Napoleon, who was elected unanimously. *(Chapter IX)*

> "'Long live Comrade Napoleon! Napoleon is always right.' Those were his very last words, comrades." *(Chapter IX)*

> … from somewhere or other the pigs had acquired the money to buy themselves another case of whisky. *(Chapter IX)*

2. Write one or two paragraphs about Orwell's use of irony in Chapter IX and how effective you think it is.

3. Find two or three further examples of Orwell's use of irony and comment on the effect it has on the reader.

Humour

Much of the humour in *Animal Farm* is due to the incongruity of animals behaving like people, but Orwell also uses jokey asides that only the reader will understand. The description of the cat, 'who was afterwards discovered to have voted on both sides' *(Chapter I)* is all the more amusing because it fits the nature of cats. The struggle of the animals to learn the alphabet is humorous, as well as touching. The idea that 'Some hams hanging in the kitchen were taken out for burial' *(Chapter II)* is funny, as is the idea of Mollie trying on ribbons in front of Mrs Jones's mirror. There are many of these touches, where animals are given human traits, as in the bracketed comment following Snowball's painting of the commandments, 'With some difficulty (for it is not easy for a pig to balance himself on a ladder) Snowball climbed up and set to work, with Squealer a few rungs below him holding the paint-pot.' *(Chapter II)* Later, Orwell writes of the pigs sending the seriously ill Boxer 'a large bottle of pink medicine which they had found in the medicine chest in the bathroom' *(Chapter IX)*. Nobody knows what it is, but the reader can guess it's for a minor ailment such as indigestion.

Orwell uses humour when he imitates the really bad poetry of Minimus and pokes fun at the kind of afterlife represented by Sugarcandy Mountain. He also satirizes civil servants when he describes, through Squealer, how 'the pigs had to expend enormous labours every day upon mysterious things called "files", "reports", "minutes" and "memoranda". These were large sheets of paper which had to be closely covered with writing, and as soon as they were so covered they were burnt in the furnace.' *(Chapter X)* Orwell's use of **anthropomorphism** enables him to mock human institutions and governments in a way that readers will understand.

Even in scenes which would not be considered amusing in themselves, there are moments where we cannot help laughing. For example, during the dreadful scene of confession and slaughter, there is something ridiculous in the accusation of two sheep 'having murdered an old ram, an especially devoted follower of Napoleon, by chasing him round and round a bonfire when he was suffering from a cough' *(Chapter VII)*. The contrast between the humorous accusation and the brutal punishment is evident.

---

anthropomorphism giving human traits and characteristics to animals

---

Tips for assessment

Upgrade

You will need to show that although it is about serious issues, you have understood how Orwell uses humour in the book, sometimes even at very dark moments. You should use short examples and evaluate the effect on the reader.

Language as propaganda

While Orwell's own prose style is lucid and comprehensible, he is very good at portraying the ways in which language can be used to conceal and deceive. This is an area he went on to explore further in his novel *1984*.

The animals are encouraged to learn the Seven Commandments by heart at the beginning, when the pigs are teaching Animalism, but they are not told of the changes made by the pigs as they break the commandments. Each infringement of the principles laid down by old Major is justified by Squealer, using logic-chopping, pseudo-science, invented figures and statistics, and downright lies, as well as threats. When the meetings are abolished, the animals are told: **"He would be only too happy to let you make your decisions for yourselves. But sometimes you might make the wrong decisions, comrades, and then where should we be?"** *(Chapter V)* None of the animals suggest that this is the nature of an equal society any more than they argue when they are told that the windmill was really Napoleon's idea and his opposition to it was 'tactics'.

Squealer is also adept at rewriting history, relying on the animals' poor memories. He insists that Snowball was in league with Jones and that Napoleon was the true hero of the Battle of the Cowshed: **"And do you not remember, too, that it was just at that moment, when panic was spreading and all seemed lost, that Comrade Napoleon sprang forward with a cry of 'Death to Humanity!' and sank his teeth in Jones's leg?"** *(Chapter VII)* Of course, the animals remember no such thing, as it never happened, but they are encouraged to see Snowball only as an evil influence, while Napoleon becomes ever more untouchable. **'He was always referred to in formal style as "our Leader, Comrade Napoleon",** and the pigs liked to invent for him such titles as Father of All Animals, Terror of Mankind, Protector of the Sheepfold, Ducklings' Friend, and the like.' *(Chapter VIII)* These grandiose titles serve to elevate Napoleon's status to that of a kind of god who cannot be questioned.

Squealer is very adept at rewriting history, as well as the commandments (in the 1954 film)

Activity 5

Look at Squealer's short speech below, which occurs after he tells the animals that singing 'Beasts of England' has been banned. The sentences have been numbered to help you.

(1) "It is no longer needed, comrade," said Squealer stiffly. (2) "'Beasts of England' was the song of the Rebellion. (3) But the Rebellion is now completed. (4) The execution of the traitors this afternoon was the final act. (5) The enemy both external and internal has been defeated. (6) In 'Beasts of England' we expressed our longing for a better society in days to come. (7) But that society has now been established. (8) Clearly this song has no longer any purpose." *(Chapter VII)*

1. What is Squealer's main argument here? How logical do you think it is?
2. How are sentences 2 and 3 mirrored by sentences 6 and 7?
3. How is sentence 1 mirrored by sentence 8?
4. How is sentence 4 reinforced by sentence 5?
5. What effect is created by this rhetorical balance?
6. What do you think Orwell wanted readers to think as they read this?

Foreshadowing

Even from the beginning of the book, in old Major's speech, Orwell uses foreshadowing. Many of the evils that old Major condemns at the start of the novel, under the humans, are there once again under the pigs at the end of the book. Events that happen earlier on, like the pigs taking the milk and apples, foreshadow their later luxurious lifestyle at the expense of the enslaved and starving animals. Napoleon's removal of the puppies to 'make himself responsible for their education' *(Chapter III)* foreshadows their use as a secret police force later, while his expulsion of Snowball foreshadows Napoleon's growth of power, partly through the use of Snowball as a scapegoat.

Activity 6

Work in a group of four, each person with a copy of old Major's speech from Chapter I. Go through it and highlight all the bad things that he claims are due to Man. Ask everyone in the group to read through Chapter II, making notes of any foreshadowing they see.

Then divide the book as follows: Person A takes Chapters III and X; person B takes Chapters IV and IX; person C takes Chapters V and VIII; person D takes Chapters VI and VII. Each person should find any references and quotations that indicate something foreshadowed in Chapters I and II.

Make a chart, on the lines of the one below, which shows clearly how Orwell foreshadows the eventual abuse of power by the pigs and the events that happen later in the story.

> **misery and slavery** (the animals under Man, Chapter I)

> **"Never mind the milk"** (Napoleon to the animals, Chapter II)

> **They were generally hungry** (the animals under the pigs, Chapter X)

> **the farm had grown richer without making the animals themselves any richer – except, of course, for the pigs and the dogs** (Chapter X)

You should show that you are aware of Orwell's use of foreshadowing and the way in which it alerts the reader to what may happen further on in the story. Give short examples and analyse what they foreshadow and why Orwell has used this technique.

Orwell's style

In *Animal Farm*, Orwell's style is direct and simple, as befits a fairy tale. The opening sentence sets the tone: '**Mr Jones, of the Manor Farm, had locked the hen-houses for the night, but was too drunk to remember to shut the pop-holes.**' *(Chapter I)* This is a direct statement, without figurative language, and is typical of Orwell's writing in general. His journalistic style has often been commented on because of his plain storytelling.

Orwell sometimes uses sentences that list things, like 'His men were idle and dishonest, the fields were full of weeds, the buildings wanted roofing, the hedges were neglected and the animals were underfed.' *(Chapter II)* This has a cumulative effect that builds up all the things that are wrong until it seems overwhelming.

When there is an exciting action sequence, Orwell creates tension with short, simple sentences using **active verbs**, such as 'The men gave a shout of triumph.' *(Chapter IV)* He also uses this simple structure when he is telling a moving part of the story, such as the animals' reactions to Napoleon's executions: 'When it was all over, the remaining animals, except for the pigs and dogs, crept away in a body. They were shaken and miserable.' *(Chapter VII)* The executions themselves are made shocking by the description of how 'the dogs promptly tore their throats out' *(Chapter VII)*, which is not only a physical act but also a symbolic one, as it literally prevents the other animals from speaking out.

The fact that Orwell is writing from a distance as an observer has the effect of heightening the reader's emotional response in a way that might not happen if the narrator were more involved with the action. His narrator is a neutral observer who does not often suggest what the animals are thinking or feeling during an action. For example, we are told that after the hens' rebellion, Napoleon 'ordered the hens' rations to be stopped, and decreed that any animal giving so much as a grain of corn to a hen should be punished by death' *(Chapter VII)*, but not how the animals reacted. He also allows the reader to deduce for themselves what to think, rather than telling them. For example, after Snowball's expulsion, he writes, 'It was noticed that they wagged their tails to him [Napoleon] in the same way as the other dogs had been used to do to Mr Jones.' *(Chapter V)* This foreshadowing of the end of the book allows readers to draw their own conclusions about what Napoleon is up to, although Orwell's use of the passive voice ('it was noticed') leaves it unclear as to *who* noticed. Orwell's use of the passive voice at key moments throughout the novel has two main purposes. First, it keeps the narrator's voice neutral, which can have a very powerful effect, as in 'Boxer was never seen again' *(Chapter IX)*; second, it leaves us guessing exactly who has noticed – the animals or the narrator? The effect of this is to make sure the reader has noticed what is happening, even when the animals haven't.

> **active verb** a verb that expresses an action, e.g. 'run' or 'throw'

Activity 7

Find two or three examples of each of the following:

a) simple direct statements that move the story forward

b) sentences that include lists of things

c) short sentences used to heighten tension in action scenes

d) short sentences used to intensify emotion

e) sentences that describe both physical and symbolic actions

f) sequences that allow readers to draw their own conclusions.

Discuss each of your examples and why you think it is effective. Make your examples and conclusions into a display for your classmates. You could add pictures, colours, different fonts, etc. to make your display noticeable.

Writing about language

Upgrade

Examiners are often disappointed that students do not write in enough detail about an author's use of language. It is very important, whatever you are asked to focus on in your assessment, that you include discussion of a writer's style and techniques in some depth, supported by references and short quotations. For example, it is not enough to comment on irony in the book – you need to show how and why Orwell has chosen to use irony for specific purposes. You should comment in detail, using short examples.

Themes

Dreams and ideals

The book opens with old Major's dream that animals will be free of human oppression and able to live in an equal society where they all own the land and work for the general good. He teaches them the song, 'Beasts of England', which expresses this 'golden future time' *(Chapter I)*. The other animals enjoy learning this song and singing it, but Orwell doesn't tell us what they think about it. It is the pigs that set about turning old Major's dream into some sort of philosophy called Animalism, with its own commandments.

When the animals succeed in driving Jones from the farm, they are jubilant and set fire to all the whips and knives and other instruments of tyranny. This euphoria lasts all through the harvest, while the animals work together. 'The animals were happy as they had never conceived it possible to be. Every mouthful of food was an acute positive pleasure, now that it was truly their own food, produced by themselves and for themselves, not doled out to them by a grudging master.' *(Chapter III)*

Even when Napoleon becomes more **despotic** and cruel than Jones ever was, the animals never seem to lose this sense of idealism: 'It might be that their lives were hard and that not all of their hopes had been fulfilled; but they were conscious that they were not as other animals. If they went hungry, it was not from feeding tyrannical human beings; if they worked hard, at least they worked for themselves. No creature among them went upon two legs. No creature called any other creature "Master". All animals were equal.' *(Chapter X)*

> **despotic** oppressive and tyrannical

Activity 1

Work with a partner.

1. Read old Major's speech at the beginning of the book. Discuss and make notes on how Orwell presents Major's dream for the future. Then do the same for 'Beasts of England'.

2. Read and make notes on how Orwell presents Clover's ideas of what the dream entailed (see Chapter VII). What similarities and differences can you find in the dreams themselves and in how Orwell shows them to the reader?

3. Discuss and make notes on what has happened to the dream by the time Clover reflects on it in Chapter VII and why you think this has happened.

4. Decide whether you think these dreams are realistic and possible, or whether they are just dreams that will never happen because of the way people (and animals) behave. What do you think Orwell is saying about this in the book?

5. Compare your notes with at least one other pair of students and modify them if you wish. Write your notes up into a useful form for revision.

Power and corruption

The great 19th-century historian, Lord Acton, wrote, 'Power tends to corrupt, and absolute power corrupts absolutely.' There are plenty of examples that show the truth of his saying and in *Animal Farm* it applies both to the humans and to the pigs.

The humans are shown as corrupt through the characters of Jones, Frederick and Pilkington. Jones takes his disappointments out on the animals and uses his power to overwork, abuse and starve them. He never considers their feelings and is aggrieved when they turn on him. Frederick and Pilkington treat their animals much the same and use Jones's misfortune to try and gain some advantage for themselves: **'At heart, each of them was secretly wondering whether he could not somehow turn Jones's misfortune to his own advantage.'** *(Chapter IV)* Later, Frederick takes advantage of Napoleon to defraud him of the timber and even invades the farm, blowing up the symbolic windmill. Pilkington is no better, for at the end of the book he and Napoleon have a row over cheating at cards.

The first sign of corruption in the pigs is when they secretly learn to read and write, and they formulate Animalism and the commandments without consulting the other animals. This might not seem so bad – after all, someone has to take the initiative – but it leads to darker things, foreshadowed by the way they keep the milk and apples for themselves. Orwell makes it clear that **'All the pigs were in full agreement on this point, even Snowball and Napoleon.'** *(Chapter III)* Squealer's explanation is the first time we see his powers of persuasion in action. The animals are not happy about it, but they accept it because none of them can think beyond not wanting Jones to come back.

Orwell wrote 'I meant the moral to be that revolutions only effect a radical improvement when the masses are alert and know how to chuck out their leaders as soon as the latter have done their job. The turning point of the story was supposed to be when the pigs kept the milk and apples for themselves [...] If the other animals had had the sense to put their foot down, it would have been all right.'

Orwell shows different forms of power in *Animal Farm*. Old Major's authority is a result of the rhetorical power of his speech and also because he has the respect of the animals. Boxer has power because of his great strength, **'more like three horses than one'** *(Chapter III)*, but sadly he is lacking the brains that would have made him a leader. He takes refuge in work and in slogans that require no thought. The pigs have power through their intelligence and better education: Snowball because he is inventive and a passionate speaker; Squealer because he can twist words and ideas to

Egyptians protest in Cairo in January 2012 for a swifter move to civilian government, waving the Egyptian flag

conceal the truth. Napoleon's power, on the other hand, is gained through his use of the dogs to kill and intimidate the other animals.

When old Major dies, the pigs use their knowledge to take control of the Rebellion. They try to educate the other animals, but most of the other animals are too stupid, with the result that they can easily be manipulated. It is soon seen that Napoleon has been preparing for a takeover and, with Snowball gone, there is no real opposition.

Activity 2

When the Rebellion first happens, Napoleon and Snowball seem to have a fairly equal share in the leadership.

Work in a group of four. Each person should take one of Chapters II, III, IV and V. Look at the following and make brief notes:

- how Orwell presents the power of humans
- what symbols of power he shows and how they are used
- how Napoleon manipulates power after the Rebellion
- how Snowball manipulates power after the Rebellion
- how Orwell shows power corrupting the pigs.

Discuss your findings and present them to other groups.

Tips for assessment

If you are answering a question for an exam board that includes context in the assessment, remember to relate your answer *briefly* not only to the corruption of communism under Stalin but also to more contemporary events, perhaps in Africa or the Middle East.

If you are not required to use context in your answer, you should remember to make any references to Orwell's intentions relevant to the novel itself.

The power of language is demonstrated by Orwell in several ways. It is shown by the effect of old Major's speech, by the formulation of the commandments and by the arguments of both Snowball and Squealer. The sheep cannot even remember the commandments, so Snowball reduces the whole philosophy to a single slogan that they can bleat meaninglessly for hours. In the end, "Four legs good, two legs bad" *(Chapter V)* becomes a tool used by Napoleon to drown out any opposition. Language is presented by Orwell as a double-edged weapon that can be used to subvert meaning, as shown when the slogan changes to "Four legs good, two legs better!" *(Chapter X)* and the commandments are altered by Squealer. The ultimate corruption of language is seen in the conversion of the final commandment to 'All animals are equal, but some animals are more equal than others.' *(Chapter X)* It is a statement that completely undermines the meaning of the word 'equal' and turns it into nonsense.

Squealer and Napoleon use language to cover up the meaning of their actions and to confuse the animals, so that something that should be a means of communication becomes a method of control.

Activity 3

1. For each of the following extracts, discuss and make notes on the role of the pigs at this stage in the story:

   a) From the start of Chapter II down to '... and led the singing of "Beasts of England" with which the meetings always ended'.

   b) Chapter V from 'Silent and terrified, the animals crept back into the barn...' down to '... in addition to his private motto of "I will work harder."'

   c) Chapter VII from 'Four days later, in the late afternoon, Napoleon ordered all the animals to assemble in the yard' to 'From now onwards it was forbidden to sing it.'

   d) The final part of the novel from Chapter X 'It was just after the sheep had returned...' to the end.

2. Imagine you have been asked to make a simple five-minute video for a website about the way in which Orwell shows the changing role of the pigs throughout the novel. You should give your own thoughts, based on the above extracts, and include appropriate references and quotations including the way the pigs justify their actions. If you wish, you could add suitable pictures and music. Film the result and upload it to the school's intranet to help other students.

Deceit and trust

Orwell said that 'pigs are the most annoying destructive animals [...] They are hard to keep out of anywhere because they are so strong and cunning.' This may be why he chose them to represent the new ruling class in *Animal Farm*.

'Cunning' is a word that describes the pigs well, especially Napoleon and Squealer. Napoleon removes the puppies in Chapter III, shortly before the decision to keep all the milk and apples is made. He tells nobody what he is doing until he launches them on Snowball in the debate over the windmill. This is well before the Battle of the Cowshed, so it is clear that Napoleon has been secretly planning his **coup d'état** for some time. The animals automatically trust the pigs, because they have led them through the learning of Animalism and the Rebellion itself. They make the mistake of assuming that the pigs' intelligence means that they are wise: **'The work of teaching and organising the others fell naturally upon the pigs, who were generally recognised as being the cleverest of the animals.'** *(Chapter II)*

coup d'état a French phrase meaning the takeover of a government

It is because the animals take what the pigs tell them at face value that they are disadvantaged. Being honest themselves, they find it hard to imagine why they should be deceived and lied to. This means that the animals seldom question what they are told, even when it seems obvious to the reader that it's a complete fabrication. For example, the animals don't seem to notice that it's those who questioned Napoleon who confess to being in league with Snowball and are then executed. The other animals believe that being in league with Snowball is evil, because they've been told he is a traitor, even though they saw for themselves at the Battle of the Cowshed that this was untrue. They trust Napoleon and Squealer, even after they have seen what happened to Snowball. They also saw Snowball draw the plans for the windmill and heard his proposals for its use, but they don't have confidence in their own observations.

> **Key quotations**
>
> Why, then, asked somebody, had he spoken so strongly against it? Here Squealer looked very sly. That, he said, was Comrade Napoleon's cunning. He had *seemed* to oppose the windmill, simply as a manoeuvre to get rid of Snowball, who was a dangerous character and a bad influence. Now that Snowball was out of the way the plan could go forward without his interference. This, said Squealer, was something called tactics. *(Chapter V)*

If the animals do disagree with what they are told, the dogs are on hand to make sure they change their minds. Boxer, who could deal with the dogs, instead adopts the motto, "Napoleon is always right" *(Chapter VI)*. This unearned trust in Napoleon gets Boxer an undeserved fate when he is sent to be killed. Even then the animals believe the tissue of lies and inventions told to them by Squealer and Napoleon about Boxer's 'touching' end: 'And when Squealer went on to give further graphic details of Boxer's death-bed, the admirable care he had received and the expensive medicines for which Napoleon had paid without a thought as to the cost, their last doubts disappeared and the sorrow that they felt for their comrade's death was tempered by the thought that at least he had died happy.' *(Chapter IX)*

Napoleon, and the other pigs, soon learned to live in the comparative luxury of the farmhouse, eating banquets from the fruits of the other animals' labours

Orwell makes the reader wonder if being ignorant and trusting is really worthy of such contempt, when the animals have given everything for the success of Animal Farm. The pigs, on the other hand, use their superior intelligence and skills, not to improve things for everyone, but to grab as much as they can for themselves. They do little work, produce large numbers of offspring and live in luxury. It seems that virtue is punished and corruption rewarded on Animal Farm. Trust is answered with deceit and loyalty with betrayal.

> **Key quotations**
>
> After that it did not seem strange when next day the pigs who were supervising the work of the farm all carried whips in their trotters. It did not seem strange to learn that the pigs had bought themselves a wireless set, were arranging to install a telephone, and had taken out subscriptions to *John Bull*, *Tit-Bits* and the *Daily Mirror*. It did not seem strange when Napoleon was seen strolling in the farmhouse garden with a pipe in his mouth – no, not even when the pigs took Mr Jones's clothes out of the wardrobes and put them on... *(Chapter X)*

Tips for assessment

If you are answering an extract-based question, it is important to refer to it in your answer. You should remember to use evidence from the extract to support the points you make. The extract is there to help you focus your answer and so you should use and evaluate quotations from it.

> ### Activity 4
>
> Find three examples of each of the following:
>
> **a)** how the animals' ignorance and trust enables the pigs to manipulate them
>
> **b)** how the pigs' acquisition of power leads to their corruption.
>
> Discuss what your examples show about Orwell's presentation of power and corruption. Create a visual display for your classroom. Divide your display into two, showing the animals' hard work and honesty and the pigs' power and corruption. You could include pictures, quotations and your own comments. Write a brief paragraph underneath about Orwell's reasons for making this an important theme of his book.

Nature of oppression

In the first chapter of the book, old Major points out that "Man is the only creature that consumes without producing. He does not give milk, he does not lay eggs, he is too weak to pull the plough, he cannot run fast enough to catch rabbits. Yet he is lord of all the animals. He sets them to work, he gives back to them the bare minimum that will prevent them from starving, and the rest he keeps for himself." This is what he sees of the oppression of animals by humans. What he doesn't foresee is that when the common enemy, Man, is driven out, this oppression will transfer itself to a different group. The pigs are already seen as the natural leaders because of their intelligence. Their secretive habits, like teaching themselves to read and write, and their evolving of old Major's speech into a whole philosophy with its own commandments, are not commented on by the animals, although the narrator shows that this lack of transparency and failure to involve all the animals will lead to darker conspiracies later on. 'These three [Napoleon, Snowball and Squealer] had elaborated old Major's teachings into a complete system of thought, to which they gave the name of Animalism.' *(Chapter II)*

Orwell presents the animals as united when they are driven by hunger and fury to turn on Jones and his men, and again at the Battle of the Cowshed. But without a common enemy, there are divisions among the animals themselves. After driving him out, Napoleon is able to create another common enemy in the form of Snowball, who can safely be blamed for everything that goes wrong on the farm. Of course, this is all lies, but the animals accept it and become fearful and easier to manipulate. While Napoleon is demonizing Snowball – an animal – he is also trading with Frederick, an old enemy, who shows his true colours by defrauding the animals and blowing up their windmill.

> **Key quotations**
>
> It now appeared that Snowball had not, as the animals had previously imagined, merely attempted to lose the Battle of the Cowshed by means of a stratagem, but had been openly fighting on Jones's side. In fact it was he who had actually been the leader of the human forces, and had charged into battle with the words "Long live Humanity!" on his lips. The wounds on Snowball's back, which a few of the animals still remembered to have seen, had been inflicted by Napoleon's teeth. *(Chapter IX)*

The animals are caught between the terror of the dogs on the farm and of Snowball, who is outside it but apparently able to infiltrate and cause damage at will. This is the way they are kept in subjection. Even when they can see the pigs getting fat while they starve, the animals are convinced that they are better off than under Jones. However, even Jones didn't make himself into a cult figure like Napoleon, who calls himself president, is accompanied everywhere by a bodyguard and reserves the best of everything for himself. Nor did Jones have the hypocrisy to sell his most loyal worker for whisky while calling himself 'Father of All Animals' *(Chapter VIII)*.

Apart from Squealer's endless propaganda, Napoleon's main tools of oppression are the dogs and the sheep. While the dogs act as a private army, the sheep are so stupid that they act only as a crowd and all bleat the same slogan when told to. Napoleon and Squealer use this noise to drown out any protest, as when the pigs walk round on their hind legs.

Key quotations

Then there came a moment when the first shock had worn off and when in spite of everything – in spite of their terror of the dogs, and of the habit, developed through long years, of never complaining, never criticising, no matter what happened – they might have uttered some word of protest. But just at that moment, as though at a signal, all the sheep burst out into a tremendous bleating of –

"Four legs good, two legs *better*! Four legs good, two legs *better*! Four legs good, two legs *better*!"

It went on for five minutes without stopping. And by the time the sheep had quieted down the chance to utter any protest had passed, for the pigs had marched back into the farmhouse. *(Chapter X)*

The inevitable end of all the greed and betrayal practised by the pigs then unfolds as they turn into the humans they had fought to break free from. They are now wearing humans' clothes, both literally and symbolically.

Activity 5

Work with a partner and discuss the following questions.

1. When the hens show their willingness to go against Napoleon, why do you think none of the other animals join in or at least give them support?

2. Why do you think the animals are so ready to believe Squealer's account of past events, when even Boxer remembers it differently?

3. When Boxer shows he is easily able to cope with the dogs, why do you think the animals watch the 'executions' without rebelling against the pigs?

4. When they know that 'Beasts of England' is their own song, why do they go along with its abolition?

5. Is there any point at which Orwell shows that the animals could have stopped the pigs? If so, why didn't they?

Put your answers in the form of a PowerPoint presentation that sums up how Napoleon and Squealer are able to dominate the farm and the animals, when they could not run it without them. You could use suitable pictures and quotations, as well as your own comments.

Religion and propaganda

Karl Marx wrote 'Religion is the sigh of the oppressed creature, the heart of a heartless world, and the soul of soulless conditions. It is the opium of the people.' He was saying that it was a way for people in misery to make sense of their condition. As such, it is no coincidence that Orwell shows Moses the raven as Jones's pet. Moses tells the animals of the 'Promised Land' of Sugarcandy Mountain, where they will go after death. He disappears with Jones but returns after Napoleon becomes a dictator and presumably encourages him to keep the animals working hard in the expectation of a better life to come. Many of the animals believe Moses: 'Their lives now, they reasoned, were hungry and laborious; was it not right and just that a better world should exist somewhere else?' *(Chapter IX)*

Like oppressed people everywhere, many African Americans in the 19th century found comfort in their religious beliefs, as shown in this illustration of a prayer meeting

On the other hand, they have Squealer telling them how much better life is getting, even though they are starving and enslaved. He gives out confusing lists of figures to prove that life is easier. 'Reading out the figures in a shrill rapid voice, he proved to them in detail that they had more oats, more hay, more turnips than they had had in Jones's day, that they worked shorter hours, that their drinking water was of better quality, that they lived longer, that a larger proportion of their young ones survived infancy, and that they had more straw in their stalls and suffered less from fleas.' *(Chapter IX)*

Activity 6

Work in a small group and discuss the following questions.

1. Why did Jones keep Moses as a pet?

2. Why did Napoleon allow him back?

3. What part in the animals' lives does Moses play?

4. How does the life he shows on Sugarcandy Mountain differ from the life the animals experience on Manor/Animal Farm?

Make brief notes on your findings and comment on why you think Orwell includes this theme in the novel.

Writing about themes

Upgrade

The way you approach themes in the exam will depend on the question you have been asked. The question(s) may be on one particular theme, such as dreams and hopes, the corruption of power or oppression. In this case you need to show how the author brings out these themes through the different characters and events.

The themes in this chapter are only some of the possibilities you may be asked about. You may be asked to consider other themes, such as change, revolution or violence, and you should be prepared to adapt your knowledge and understanding as required.

Even if the question is not specifically about themes in the novel, you should still show that you have understood them. For example, if you are writing about the character of Snowball, you can show how Orwell presents ideas about leadership, trust, violence and dreams through the way in which Snowball behaves, what he says, what we are told about him by the narrator and what happens to him, as well as how he is remembered.

You should also look at how a theme develops as the book progresses. For example, do power and corruption become more important at the end of the book than at the beginning? Do certain events in the story make the theme more dominant? For example, does the scene in which Boxer is taken away bring trust to the foreground? How is oppression shown at different times in the story by and towards different characters?

Remember, examiners are looking for your own response to and opinions about the novel, based on what you have learned.

Exam skills

Understanding the question

Look at the number of marks awarded to each section of the question. Then divide the time you have available for the answer in proportion to the marks. For example, if you have 45 minutes to answer a two-part question where part a) is worth 7 marks and part b) is worth 20 marks, it is clear you should spend no more than ten minutes on part a) and 30 minutes on part b), allowing five minutes for planning. If the two parts are worth 10 marks each, you should aim to spend 20 minutes on each part.

Try to approach the question in a methodical way. Start by identifying what the question is actually asking you to do. You could do this by underlining the key words and phrases, and writing in what they mean. Examiners use certain words and phrases quite often. Learn what they mean and that will tell you what you need to write about.

'**Explore**' means look at all the different aspects of something. For example, 'Explore the significance of trust...' means you need to look at who trusts whom in the book and whether this trust is justified or not; why characters are trusted and whether they are worthy of it or not; how trust is shown and what response is made to it; and how important the trust, or lack of it, is to the plot, structure and themes of the story.

If you are required to consider context in the assessment, you should show briefly how people tend to trust their leaders, especially following the Russian revolution, which was in the name of equality.

'**How does the author...**' or '**show how...**' means explain the techniques the author uses to gain an effect. For example, 'How does Orwell make this episode tense?' means you need to look at how he builds up suspense or tension in the way he structures the episode; how he uses language such as verbs and descriptions to make the reader feel excitement or fear; how he uses the reactions of various characters to convey their emotions.

'**Present**' and '**portray**' are similar words for looking at a character and they prompt you to consider not only what the character is like, but also what devices the author uses to show us this. For example, 'How is Squealer presented/portrayed?' means you need to think about how he is described; what the author makes him say and do, and why; how the author reveals the reactions of other characters; and how Orwell shows the character as important to the story as a whole.

You could also briefly explain how Stalin used the Russian newspaper *Pravda* to mislead the workers into thinking that everything was going well and the economy was improving, when the opposite was the case, and how this relates to Squealer in the book. You should also relate this to society in general and the way the media can manipulate opinion.

'**In what ways...**' means look at different sides of something. For example, 'In what ways is the relationship between Napoleon and Snowball important?' means that you need to look at the way they formulate Animalism and the commandments together with Squealer. You need to explain their function as representing two different ways of using power, and how their disagreement about everything leads to a power struggle in which Napoleon is victorious. You also need to evaluate how the demonizing of Snowball keeps the animals in fear and makes them easier to manage, as well as how it provides Napoleon with a convenient scapegoat for anything that goes wrong.

You may also briefly explain how this is related to the way in which Stalin (Napoleon) and Trotsky (Snowball) worked together with Lenin for the Russian revolution. You should mention how they disagreed after Lenin's death about how to take the Russian economy forward and how Trotsky was exiled and later murdered by the KGB. You could also relate this to society in general and how those prepared to use violence can take control.

'**How far...**' means the examiner wants you to show the extent of something. For example, 'How far is the animals' lack of education to blame for Napoleon becoming a dictator?' means that you need to think about how Orwell presents the animals as being too stupid to stand up for themselves; how he presents the violence used by Napoleon as being too great to stand against; how he shows the use of outside threats like Snowball and Jones to inspire fear and obedience; and overall whether it is lack of education or the other influences that are most important.

You could also explain how the animals represent the peasants and workers in Russia, who were often illiterate and were manipulated and repressed by Stalin and the KGB. You could also relate this to society in general and the way in which people are at the mercy of those in power.

'**What role...**' prompts you to think about the importance of a character and the character's function in the novel. For example, 'What role does Snowball play?' means you need to consider Snowball's character and how it is conveyed in the novel, but also why he is in the novel at all. You could try to imagine the novel without him – he is an inventive and intelligent character who leads the Battle of the Cowshed and reveals the possibility of a better life for all the animals. He is the cleverest of all the pigs, but he shows that cleverness cannot overcome physical violence, especially when unexpected. His later role is created for him by Napoleon – as the scapegoat and traitor who becomes a hate figure.

You could also explain how Snowball stands for Leon Trotsky, the inspiring leader who disagreed with Stalin and was exiled to Mexico, where he was later assassinated by the KGB. You may wish to relate this to society in general, showing how the media and those in power can create a false impression of those who are openly critical.

'**Explain**' or '**comment on**' are phrases that invite you to give your response to something in as much detail as you can. For example, 'Explain the importance of the windmill in the novel' means you should write about the way in which the plans show the difference in leadership between Napoleon and Snowball and the potential improvements to the animals' lives that might have resulted. You also need to write about how it provides the final excuse for Snowball's expulsion; how it was taken over by Napoleon and used as a method for keeping the animals too hard at work to question his authority; how its destruction by the storm begins the demonizing of Snowball; and the effect on the animals when it is blown up by Frederick. All these factors help to show its importance as a central symbol in the novel.

You could also explain how the windmill is a symbolic representation of the implementation of Stalin's five-year plans. Similarly, its explosion, followed by the Battle of the Windmill, represents the German attack on Moscow. You may also wish to relate this to society in general and the way in which leaders manipulate people into working for a common cause, which blinds them to other things that the government is doing (e.g. taking part in a foreign war).

Look at the question below. The key words and phrases have been highlighted and explained.

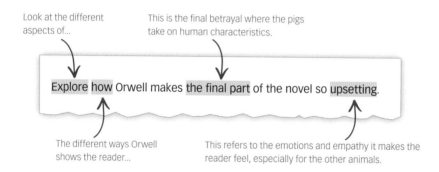

Look at the different aspects of...

This is the final betrayal where the pigs take on human characteristics.

Explore how Orwell makes the final part of the novel so upsetting.

The different ways Orwell shows the reader...

This refers to the emotions and empathy it makes the reader feel, especially for the other animals.

You can see that you are being asked to do a number of things in this question. You need to look at the methods Orwell uses to:

- bring out the relationship between the pigs and the humans
- show the reader the animals' feelings
- show the pigs' complete betrayal of the Rebellion
- make the reader aware of the way things have come full circle.

Tips for assessment

Upgrade

To reach the higher marks, you need to show that you have thought about the book for yourself and can give your own opinions about what the author is saying and how he is saying it, supporting your ideas with relevant references and quotations.

Activity 1

1. Write out the following question.

   Explore the importance of hopes and dreams within the novel as a whole.

   a) Highlight or underline the key words and phrases and then describe what you are being asked to do.

   b) Make a bullet list of things you need to do to answer the question.

2. Work with a partner and imagine you are the Chief Examiner. Write two or three questions that you think would test the assessment objectives for this part of the exam. Try to word them as they would be on an actual paper. Check the website of your exam board to find example questions and a list of the assessment objectives.

3. Swap with another pair and analyse each other's questions as in the exemplar above.

Planning your answer

It is worth taking five minutes to plan your answer before you start to write it. It means you will have the information you need in front of you and you will have some kind of structure for your response. You will be free to concentrate on your writing style and on making sure you have used the correct terminology and included evidence to support your points.

Examiners always make the point that candidates who use their own ideas about the text produce fresher and more interesting answers than candidates who have prepared essays in advance. So, the key is to practise planning answers to a variety of questions.

You can make a list of points you want to include, making sure that each point focuses on the question. You may also wish to include a brief note of the evidence you will use for each point in your response. The table on page 80 shows what a detailed list might look like for the following question:

Explore how Orwell makes the final part of the novel so upsetting.

Techniques (how)	Effects (why it is upsetting)
1. Introduction – the relationship between the animals when they are inspired by old Major	1. Shows how the pigs sadly lost the ideals they started out with
2. The irony of the pigs being the leaders of the Rebellion and creating the commandments	2. Creates sympathy for the animals who are being exploited
3. The way Orwell shows how very different things are at the end of the novel	3. Creates a feeling of pessimism in the reader because it is a circle of violence
4. The way that the other animals finally realize that humans and pigs are no different	4. The original oppressors (humans) and the new oppressors (pigs) are shown to be the same, which suggests that power will always have this effect
5. The quick progression from pig to human (two legs, clothes, telephones, etc.)	5. The animals seem helpless to do anything – they are too old, too stupid or unaware of the Rebellion and its ideals
6. How Orwell shows the corruption of language in the single commandment reflecting the total corruption of the pigs	6. Acts as a warning about allowing any group to take too much power
7. Foreshadowing – how Orwell has made it inevitable by earlier events in the novel	7. The reader sees a chain of cause and effect
8. The reactions of the animals	8. The reader feels pity for the hard-working animals who still have nothing

The above list is an example of a detailed outline for an exam response and would probably take too long to write in an exam. You should try to have an outline in your head and summarize it into a few key words when compiling your plan.

You could also use a simple spider diagram to plan your points.

Activity 2

1. Create a spider diagram or a two-column list-style plan for each of the following questions.

   a) How does Orwell create a sense of insecurity and fear in *Animal Farm*?

   b) Look at the passage in Chapter VIII, beginning 'Three days later there was a terrible hullabaloo...' down to '... as though the windmill had never been'. In what ways does Orwell build up tension in this extract?

   c) How important do you consider the character of Boxer to be in *Animal Farm*?

   d) Look at old Major's speech in Chapter I. How well does this set the scene for everything that happens afterwards?

2. In groups of two or three, compare the plans you have created. Exchange ideas and add to or amend your plans as necessary. Add stars next to what you consider to be the most important points in each plan. Be prepared to discuss your ideas with the class.

Tips for assessment

- Plan your time carefully in the exam. Don't spend too long on your plan or you will run out of time to complete your answer.

- Don't cross out your plan, because if you do run out of time you may be given credit for it.

Writing your answer

Once you have a plan, you will have a clear idea of what you need to write to answer the question effectively. It might be helpful to prioritize your points by highlighting the ones you would like to cover first. You could do this by numbering your points in order of importance. You should also try to have an idea in mind of how you intend to finish your answer.

You need to pay close attention to the quality of your writing in your answer, including your spelling, grammar and punctuation. Your answer should show your knowledge and understanding of:

- what the author is saying
- how the author is saying it
- how the setting and (if required by your exam board) the context influence writer and reader.

Using PEE (Point, Evidence, Explanation)

Examiners want to see that you are able to support your ideas and that you have based them on what the writer says and means. For example, you might make the **point**:

> The procession of pigs walking on two legs is the final point in the book when Orwell suggests the animals might have rebelled against the pigs.

Your **evidence** for this might be:

> 'Then there came a moment when the first shock had worn off and when in spite of everything – in spite of their terror of the dogs, and of the habit, developed through long years, of never complaining, never criticising, no matter what happened – they might have uttered some word of protest.'

Your **explanation** might be:

> This shows that the animals had not completely forgotten the ideals of the Rebellion and that, even now, they could be pushed too far. The way in which Napoleon and Squealer deal with any possibility of protest is shown in the way the animals are drowned out by the sheep, the mindless followers.

Tips for assessment

Upgrade

While PEE is a helpful reminder of what you need to build into your writing, you do not need to follow this pattern for every single point you make. To reach the higher marks, you need to control your argument and try to keep your answer flowing.

Using quotations

This is an important part of using evidence in your answer. The examiner will want to see that you are able to select appropriate quotations. When you make a point, ask yourself: 'How do I know this?' Usually it will be because of something the author has written – this is the quotation you need.

For example, you might make the point:

> Old Major is well respected by everyone on the farm and they all look up to him.

You could use a number of quotations such as:

> 'Old Major [...] was so highly regarded on the farm that everyone was quite ready to lose an hour's sleep in order to hear what he had to say.'

By choosing this quotation you will show several things:

- You can select a relevant quotation to support your answer.
- You have understood how old Major is respected and others defer to him.
- You have understood that this relates to an important trait of the character.

To show skills of a higher level, try to use **embedded quotations**. These short quotations (usually of words or phrases) are easy to build into the flow of your own writing and you can also analyse them closely. For example:

> Boxer is admired by the animals for his great strength and hard work because, in spite of Squealer's speeches, '... the other animals found more inspiration in Boxer's strength and his never-failing cry of "I will work harder!"'

Embedded quotations appear within the main text of your writing and they use quotation marks in the usual way.

> **embedded quotation** short quotation of words or phrases that you can build into the flow of your writing

What not to do in an exam answer

- ✗ Do not begin with introductions such as 'In this answer I am going to show...'. Instead just start straight in and do the showing as you go. Make sure your introduction addresses the question and go back to it in your conclusion.

- ✗ Do not write lengthy paragraphs about the background to the novel. You may think the Russian revolution is important to the portrayal of the animals in the novel, but you should show this while you are answering the question itself.

- ✗ Do not write a long introduction showing what you know about the author. Make just a brief reference and only if it is relevant to a point you are making. For example, you may think Orwell's experiences in the Spanish Civil War had a profound effect on the way he shows the animals during the Rebellion and the disillusionment afterwards, but mention this as briefly as possible.

- ✗ If you are answering an extract-based question, do not focus on some parts of the set extract and ignore others. You should always answer on the passage as a whole.

- ✗ If you are answering an extract-based question, do not answer on other parts of the novel outside the extract set, except for brief references where necessary, unless you are asked to do so.

✗ Do not go into the exam with a prepared list of points and write about them regardless of whether they are relevant to the question.

✗ Do not 'feature spot'. For example, there is little merit in saying that Orwell uses symbolism without showing how he does this and what effect it creates.

✗ Do not run out of time to finish your answer – a plan will help you to avoid this.

✗ Do not try to write everything you know about the text. Make sure that you only choose things that are relevant to the question.

Achieving the best marks

Upgrade

To achieve high marks, you will need to do the following:

- Show an assured or perceptive understanding of themes/ideas.
- Show a suitable or convincing response to the text.
- Ensure your selection of evidence is relevant, detailed and consistent.
- If required, ensure that your references to context are appropriate and convincing, and supported by relevant textual reference.
- Use sentences that are sophisticated and varied; show good control of expression and meaning; use a full range of punctuation and ensure spelling is accurate.

In practice, this means that you need to read more than the text. Ideally, you need to read some critical guides to the text, and add their interpretation to your own response and ideas about the book.

In addition, you need to show that you have understood the book on more than one level. On the surface, it is a story about how a group of farm animals rebel against their human master and take over the farm, and their subsequent betrayal by their new leaders, the pigs. On an underlying level, it is a criticism of society and the way in which it fails to promote equality and freedom for all and, in particular, the betrayal of socialist ideals by Stalin in the Soviet Union. On a still deeper level, it is a novel about the human condition and the way in which evil so often seems to triumph over good (the opposite of the fairy tale!).

You will also have to show an awareness of the author's techniques. You need to show that you understand the narrative structure, such as why Orwell chose to use an omniscient narrator's viewpoint. You will also need to show not just that you have understood the symbolism that Orwell uses, but how, in your view, he applies it and why he uses it.

You will need to use the correct literary terminology to make your answers more precise and show that you have a sophisticated writing style.

Sample questions

1

Animal Farm

Answer all parts of the question.

Spelling, punctuation and grammar will be assessed in part c).

Read the extract from Chapter V, beginning 'In the long pasture, not far from the farm buildings, there was a small knoll...' to '... then suddenly he lifted his leg, urinated over the plans and walked out without uttering a word'.

Then answer the following questions:

a) From the extract, what do you discover about the character of Snowball? Use **evidence** from the extract to support your answer.

b) Explore how the writer uses language in the extract to present aspirations. Use **evidence** from the extract to support your answer.

c) In the extract Snowball becomes excited about the windmill. Explore how the writer presents the importance of the windmill in **one other** part of the novel. Use **evidence** from the extract to support your answer.

2

Animal Farm

EITHER

1. How does Orwell present Benjamin the donkey in the novel? How does Orwell use Benjamin to comment on members of society who see change as impossible?

OR

2. How does Orwell use the Seven Commandments to show the ways in which the Rebellion changes? How does Orwell use the commandments to comment on the rules of society?

3

Animal Farm

Answer all parts of the question.

Spelling, punctuation and grammar will be assessed in part c).

Read the extract from Chapter VI, beginning 'But it was a slow, laborious process...' to '... which saved a lot of labour on the upkeep of hedges and gates'.

Then answer the following questions:

a) From this extract, what do you learn about the character of Boxer? Use **evidence** from the extract to support your answer.

b) Explain how the writer uses language in the extract to show Boxer's strength and hard work. Use **evidence** from the extract to support your answer.

c) In the extract Boxer is shown as trusting Napoleon. Explain how the writer presents trust in **one other** part of the novel. Use **evidence** from the extract to support your answer.

4

Animal Farm

EITHER

1. How does Orwell present Squealer in the novel? How is he used to present ideas about society?

OR

2. How does Orwell show the themes of trust and betrayal? How do these themes reflect ideas about society?

5

Animal Farm

EITHER

1. In what ways does Orwell present Napoleon in the novel? How does his character raise questions about leadership in society?

OR

2. How does Orwell show different dreams and ideals in the novel? How do these reflect ideas about society?

6

GEORGE ORWELL: *Animal Farm*

Read the extract from Chapter X, beginning 'As for the others, their life, so far as they knew, was as it had always been...' to 'All animals were equal.'

EITHER

1 a) What do you think makes this an interesting moment in the novel?

OR

1 b) Explore the ways in which Orwell makes Snowball a significant character in the novel.

Remember to support your ideas with details from the novel.

7

GEORGE ORWELL: *Animal Farm*

Read the extract from Chapter II, beginning 'This was early in March...' to '... clover was in season all the year round, and lump sugar and linseed cake grew on the hedges'.

EITHER

1 a) How does Orwell present the relationship between the pigs and the other animals here?

OR

1 b) How important do you consider are the ideas represented by Mollie and Moses in the novel?

Remember to support your ideas with details from the book.

Activity 3

1. Choose one of the sample questions on pages 85–87. Make a plan for your answer, using one of the methods shown in the planning section (pages 79–81).

2. Choose one of the points you identified in your plan and write down how you would use PEE in your answer to show skills of selecting and evaluating evidence.

3. Find another student in your class who has chosen the same sample question and exchange notes and ideas.

Sample answers

Sample answer 1

Below is a sample answer from a student, together with examiner comments, to the following general question on the novel:

> What part does the theme of power and corruption play in the novel? Remember to use details from the novel in your answer.

The theme of power is very important in this book, because Orwell wrote it to show what happens when a group like the pigs get control over the other animals. At first the pigs use their intelligence to try and teach the other animals and persuade them to learn about Animalism. They make up the Seven Commandments to help them but only a few of the animals can learn them and hardly any learn to read. The other animals look up to the pigs because they are clever and good with words. The pigs have all the best ideas and the other animals mostly do as they are told.

Good point about writer's intentions in the novel.

Gives evidence in form of a reference and explains what happens without evaluating it.

When the pigs realize the other animals will follow them, they start to take advantage like keeping the milk and apples for themselves and telling the animals they need them for their brains. It is Squealer's job to explain this and the animals believe him especially when he says that if the pigs don't stay healthy then Jones will come back. This is the one thing the animals are scared of, so they stop arguing and let the pigs get away with it. This is the first sign of corruption, when the pigs stop being equal with the other animals, although one of the commandments says that 'All animals are equal.'

Shows understanding of the turning point but needs development.

Good use of embedded quotation but without linking it to old Major's speech.

After this, the pigs take more power, as they know Squealer will be able to make things all right with the animals by inventing good reasons and threatening that Jones will come back. There is even a power struggle among the pigs themselves as Snowball and Napoleon disagree about everything, especially the windmill. Snowball thinks it could make the animals' lives easier by driving farm machinery. Napoleon does not seem interested but when Snowball wins the debate he calls his huge fierce dogs to chase him off the farm. As soon as he has gone, Napoleon bans the debates and says there will be orders instead. Now he has the dogs he can do whatever he wants and the animals are too scared to protest.

This is a perceptive point about the politics of power, which could have been developed.

Shows understanding but could have been linked to Napoleon's premeditated removal of the puppies and a reference to the way the dogs treated him like Jones.

From then on, Napoleon is like a dictator and he takes more and more power and privileges for the pigs, and the other animals become more like slaves. The pigs start breaking the commandments one by one and then Squealer alters them with paint and tells the animals that it was always that way and they don't remember correctly. The sheep start bleating "Four legs good, two legs bad", every time it seems like an animal might protest. Napoleon is ruthless with any creature that goes against him, like when the hens rebel and he starves them until they agree. He also has a big session where his dogs murder a lot of animals who were supposed to be in league with Snowball. The other animals are very frightened and depressed by this, and when they sing 'Beasts of England' for comfort they are told it has been banned.

The point shows understanding of Napoleon's reign of terror but fails to show how it is part of the demonizing of Snowball and his use as a scapegoat.

Napoleon is clever and he uses Snowball as an excuse to justify his violence and to keep the animals afraid of him and of Jones. Even though they don't have much food, they work harder than ever, because they still think they are working for themselves rather than humans. This is a view that Napoleon and Squealer want them to have and they organize lots of parades and singing to make the animals forget they are really miserable slaves. Meanwhile, the pigs do all the things Animalism said was wrong, like drinking whisky, sleeping in the farmhouse and trading with humans.

Good point that shows perception but it needs further explanation about the importance of symbols and pride to the animals.

Shows understanding of what the pigs were doing but needs to evaluate the gradual process of corruption shown.

By the end of the book, after they've sold poor Boxer to the knackers and lied about it to the animals, the pigs start wearing clothes and walking on two legs – even carrying whips. They have turned into the humans they wanted to get rid of at the start and the animals cannot tell the difference between one lot and the other. There is only one commandment left that they haven't got rid of and it now says 'All animals are equal but some animals are more equal than others', which is nonsense because you can't have 'more equal'.

Good use of embedded quotation and good attempt at explaining language use. It needs further evaluation and linking to other incidents.

So I think the theme of power and corruption is very important to the book – you might say it is what the story is all about. Orwell saw how the Russian revolution was taken over by Stalin and how he behaved, while pretending that everyone was equal. He thought Stalin was worse than Tsar Nicholas II. This is shown by the fact that the pigs become even worse than Mr Jones had been.

Good attempt at a conclusion that refers back to the question but it needs taking further to link with contextual ideas.

Overall the candidate shows a good understanding of the question and engagement with the novel. There is some attempt to support points with evidence and quotations are appropriate and embedded. As far as analytical skills are concerned, there is some attempt to develop points in detail, but this does not go far enough, and references and quotations are not really evaluated. It would have been clearer if the candidate had used the key words 'power' and 'corruption' more often during the course of the answer to show which they were writing about when.

Sample answer 2

Below is an extract from a sample answer from a student, together with examiner comments, to the following passage-based question on the novel:

> Read the extract from Chapter VIII beginning 'A few days later...' to '... give Napoleon the credit for every successful achievement and every stroke of good fortune'.
>
> How does Orwell bring out the nature of Napoleon's leadership in this passage?

The passage begins with the aftermath of Napoleon's 'purge' of the so-called sympathizers of Snowball, who has been turned into an enemy by the pigs. It just happens that the 'traitors' are those who have shown opposition to Napoleon. As in previous cases when the pigs have broken a commandment, it seems that the animals' memories are at fault, since neither Clover nor Muriel had any recollection of the ban on killing having the words 'without cause' added. This apparently explains that even the brutal slaughter by Napoleon is justified. The commandments themselves were plain and straightforward, and based on old Major's principles. They cannot be misunderstood, but they can be altered subtly, by the addition of a suitable phrase. Orwell shows how relatively simple it is to use language in a way that confuses the original meaning. Of course, it is Squealer who is responsible for this underhand twisting of the commandments. He is found by a broken ladder with a paintbrush in the middle of the night. Only Benjamin sees the significance of this episode, but it is made clear to the reader that the pigs are rewriting the commandments to suit themselves.

Reference to what has preceded the opening is linked to the question.

Good point relating the passage to previous similar events.

Perceptive comment on Orwell's use of language.

Shows awareness of the differences in viewpoint created between the animals and the reader.

Napoleon's reign of terror, which began with the expulsion of Snowball, has turned into an unquestioned dictatorship, which he maintains with the help of the dogs, who inspire terror, and Squealer, who uses propaganda to prove that all is well and getting better. Squealer succeeds by reading out lists of figures showing 'that the production of every class of foodstuff had increased...'. Orwell is making the point that it is not only language that can be abused, but statistics. These are a favourite way for those in power to pull the wool over people's eyes, as they have no way of disproving them. Despite working far harder than under Jones, because of the need to rebuild the

Concisely summarized account of Napoleon's position.

Well-made point about Orwell's use of the animals to draw larger political parallels.

Sophisticated use of embedded quotations to support point.

Evaluation shown through use of another quotation.

Well-made point relating memory to propaganda and education.

Thoughtful evaluation of Orwell's purpose in writing the novel.

Shows awareness of novel as allegory.

Clever use of embedded quotations to show how Orwell suggests Napoleon's distance as a leader and use of royal privileges.

Shows a clear understanding of Orwell's use of irony.

Clear statement, supported by evidence, of writer's use of language for effect.

Perceptive point about one way in which Orwell uses humour.

windmill, the animals 'saw no reason to disbelieve' Squealer because they 'could no longer remember very clearly what conditions had been like' before. This attitude can be summed up by Boxer's slogan, "Napoleon is always right."

Their faulty memory is what makes it hard for the animals to be educated and is one reason why Napoleon is able to stay in power, as he and Squealer rewrite history to show the heroism of Napoleon, the villainy of Snowball and the general improvement in living conditions. Orwell is using the pigs to show how any regime can seize and retain power by using a mixture of terror and propaganda, and ensuring that the population – the animals – have no access to other information.

The other way in which Orwell shows the nature of Napoleon's leadership here is in the cult of personality, based on that of Joseph Stalin. Napoleon is presented, much like his namesake, as a kind of emperor with his 'retinue of dogs' and the cockerel who acts as 'a kind of trumpeter'. These are the trappings of royalty, as are the 'separate apartments from the others' and the fact that he is waited on by the dogs and uses 'the Crown Derby dinner service', which even the Joneses saved for special occasions in a 'glass cupboard in the drawing-room'. All these are indications of his superiority, not only over the other animals, but over the other pigs. Orwell ironically presents Napoleon (Stalin) as living like Jones (Tsar Nicholas II). This idea is continued in the way in which Napoleon is now titled. He is "our Leader, Comrade Napoleon", and has other titles as well, such as 'Father of All Animals', although the animals are unaware of the irony.

The supreme hypocrisy that is shown by Napoleon and Squealer is breathtaking. Their pretence that Napoleon is characterized by 'the deep love he bore to all animals everywhere', which Squealer delivers with 'tears rolling down his cheeks', even as they reduce the animals' rations and double their workload, has an effect on the reader. First, it makes the reader sympathetic to the animals, while feeling angry at their exploitation. Second, it is so extreme that it provokes laughter at the notion of Napoleon as the 'Ducklings' Friend' – or anyone else's for that matter.

The candidate has shown a sophisticated understanding of the novel and of the author's intentions and techniques. Quotations are well chosen, embedded and evaluated, and the passage is related briefly to context and to other parts of the novel in a thoughtful manner. There is specific reference to language use and to the novel as allegory.

Sample answer 3

Below is an extract from a sample answer from a student, together with examiner comments, to the following passage-based question on the novel:

> Read the extract from Chapter I, beginning 'Man is the only creature that consumes without producing...' to '... All animals are equal.'
>
> How does Orwell use these ideas as the basis for all the events that follow in the novel?

This extract is taken from old Major's speech to the animals at the start of the novel. It is this that makes them think about, and then work towards, the Rebellion. Without this, there would be no story and the farm would have continued as it was. Orwell is making the point that it is great thinkers, like Karl Marx, and their ideas that inspire social and political change. This extract contains the essential principles of Animalism and the Seven Commandments, which are later developed by the pigs. It's because we see the pigs as idealists and creators actively working for the other animals and for the Rebellion that we can appreciate how far they have betrayed their own principles.

Brief but relevant reference to context and a perceptive point.

Concise and relevant summary of the author's intentions and effectiveness.

It is also a foreshadowing of the way the animals' lives will be under Napoleon, just as they are under Jones. This is shown in one example by the reference to Boxer and his fate: '... the very day that those great muscles of yours lose their power, Jones will sell you to the knacker.' The horrible irony is that in spite of the Rebellion and his endless, loyal hard work, this is precisely what happens to Boxer under the pigs.

This is a well-made point supported by a relevant embedded quotation and evaluated perceptively.

Old Major's speech is not only a recital of the sufferings of animals under the rule of humans – it becomes a summary of their sufferings under the pigs at the end of the novel as well. The events of the story begin here with the prospect of a new dawn for all animals. If they overthrow their human tyrants, there will be freedom and equality for all and 'the produce of our labour would be our own'. At first this is what happens. The animals discover how to work the farm together and for their own benefit, and all decisions are debated and voted upon in a democratic fashion. However, it quickly becomes clear that the pigs will take advantage of their superior intelligence and leadership skills to claim privileges. It begins in a small way with

Perceptive reference to the last sentence of the novel.

Well-summarized reference to the dream of freedom at the start.

Shows understanding of the author's intentions and refers to Orwell's own views on novel.

the milk and the apples. The other animals are not happy with this, but instead of standing firm they allow Squealer's specious arguments to fool them. This, as Orwell himself has said, is the turning point in the novel when the animals could have stopped the pigs, but didn't.

Perceptive comments on Napoleon's character supported by appropriate references.

Shows good understanding of cause and effect in the structure of the novel.

It is soon very obvious to the reader, if not to the animals, that Napoleon, at least, has little interest in democracy. His leadership in the Rebellion has been hiding self-interest, which is shown in his instant appropriation of the milk, followed by his taking of the puppies for 'educational' purposes. No sooner has he removed Snowball, the only challenger to his power, than he bans debates and replaces them with orders. From then on, it is only a matter of time before the commandments are being broken, the animals terrorized into working like slaves and Napoleon becoming ever more 'human'.

Pertinent comment on Benjamin's character, supported by relevant references.

Shows perception of author's technique and intentions with overall view of the animals.

The only animal who is aware of what's really happening is Benjamin, but he knows the other animals won't believe him if he tries to warn them. On the one occasion he does try – when Boxer is being taken away – it's not long before Squealer has convinced them that appearances are wrong and that Boxer received great care until he died. Orwell succeeds in a difficult task – that of showing the animals as both stupid and exploited, thus eliciting the reader's impatience and sympathy in equal measure.

Good use of embedded quotations to make points about old Major as an idealist.

Relevant contextual reference that helps to relate thinkers to actual political and social events.

While the pigs live a life of ease and luxury reminiscent of old Major's portrait of Man, 'He does not give milk, he does not lay eggs, he is too weak to pull the plough...', the animals are overworked and underfed, told lies by Squealer and frightened by the dogs. Old Major's brave words, 'Only get rid of Man, and the produce of our labour would be our own. Almost overnight we could become rich and free...' take on a hollow ring when compared with the reality of Napoleon's rule. The flaw in the great thinker's plans becomes plain, for there is nothing about how to react if the animals work against their own kind. Old Major simply assumes that animals, unlike humans, will cooperate for equality and a better life for all, just as Marx assumed the workers would do once they owned the means of production.

Overall this is a well-written and perceptive answer that shows a keen understanding of the structure of the novel and the author's techniques. It relates the events and themes briefly to context. References and quotations are relevant and are evaluated where appropriate.

Glossary

active verb a verb that expresses an action, e.g. 'run' or 'throw'

allegory an extended comparison in which events and characters represent other things

allies nations bound by treaties to help each other in time of war

alliteration the repetition of the same letter or sound in words close to each other, e.g. 'I have had...'

anecdote a short story that illustrates a point, e.g. Major's story about the 'Beasts of England' song

Animalism the name that Orwell gives to the philosophy underpinning the Rebellion; it corresponds to the terms *Marxism, communism* or *socialism*

anthropomorphism giving human traits and characteristics to animals

assonance the repetition of vowel sounds, e.g. '... boil you down for the foxhounds...'

authoritarian favouring obedience to authority over personal freedom

capitalism a political system where everything is owned by individuals or corporations working to make a profit

class system a way of grouping people according to birth, income or education

cliché an unoriginal phrase that has been over-used

coalition an agreement between different groups to work together in a common interest

Cold War a phrase invented by Orwell to describe the state of military and political stand-off that existed between West and East. There were threats and tensions, but neither side could risk another real war

colonial rule the ruling of a country as a colony of another country

communism a political system in which everything is owned by the state on behalf of the people

counterpart person or thing which corresponds to or has the same function as another

coup d'état a French phrase meaning the takeover of a government

democracy a system of government that allows everyone to express their views

depose remove from power forcibly

despotic oppressive and tyrannical

dictatorship government by a single leader with total power

dramatic irony when the reader/audience know something the characters do not (e.g. in *Romeo and Juliet* the audience know Juliet isn't dead, but her family doesn't know)

embedded quotation short quotation of words or phrases that you can build into the flow of your writing

fable a story with a moral in which animals are the main characters and often substituted for humans (e.g. 'the Tortoise and the Hare')

false logic statements that appear to be logical on the surface, but do not stand up to examination

fascism a political system where all control is in the hands of a dictator

figurative language language that uses figures of speech, such as comparisons, to take the meaning beyond the literal use of the words, e.g. 'pull your socks up' used figuratively means that you need to make more effort

foil something that acts as an opposite

foreshadowing a literary technique where the author includes clues for the reader about what will happen later on

four-minute warning the amount of time that would elapse between a nuclear missile being launched and its arrival at its target

idealism believing in high ideals and noble goals

idealist someone who is influenced by ideals rather than practical considerations

ideologies the sets of ideas and beliefs of groups or political parties

Iron Curtain a metaphor used by Winston Churchill among others to describe the border defences that separated East and West in Europe

irony the opposite of what is meant or expected

KGB *Komitet gosudarstvennoy bezopasnosti*, the state security force, used by Stalin as his secret police

knacker a person who buys and slaughters horses and then sells the meat, bones and hides

maxim a saying that is connected to a truth about life or a rule about behaviour

metaphor a comparison of one thing to another to make a description more vivid; a metaphor states that one thing *is* another

moral a lesson about life or behaviour

myth a traditional or legendary story

mythic suggesting a myth (a traditional or legendary story)

non-aggression pact a treaty between countries agreeing not to go to war with each other but to settle any differences peaceably

omniscient narrator a narrator who knows the thoughts and feelings of all the characters and can tell the story from multiple viewpoints

onomatopoeia the formation of words that sound like the things they describe

passive voice this is the opposite of the active voice and focuses on the thing rather than the action, e.g. 'it was noticed' rather than 'the animals noticed'

proletariat the ordinary or working-class people who sell their labour for wages

propaganda the deliberate spreading of ideas or information that promote the interests of a particular group

regime an authoritarian government

rhetorical question question that either does not need an answer or to which the answer is provided immediately by the speaker

satire a form of expression or literary work in which vices, follies, abuses and shortcomings are exaggerated or held up to ridicule, with the intention of reforming the person or society being mocked

satirical in which humour or exaggeration is used to show the vices, follies, abuses and shortcomings of a person or thing

Seven Commandments these are roughly comparable with the Ten Commandments of the Old Testament and lay down a set of rules for a just society

simile a comparison that uses 'like' or 'as', e.g. 'bright as a button'

situational irony when the outcome of an event/action is the reverse of that expected (e.g. being hit by lightning after carefully avoiding trees)

slogan a motto expressing the aims of a group

socialism a political system where land, property and essential services are run by an elected government on behalf of the people

Soviet Union a former communist country, which included Russia and 14 other republics

Spanish Civil War fought between 1936 and 1939, it is often seen as a 'rehearsal' for the Second World War. General Franco sought to establish a fascist military dictatorship in Spain, supported by Hitler's Germany. He was opposed by communist and socialist forces supported by the International Brigades, which were made up of young men from all over the world who supported the anti-fascist cause

symbolism using objects to represent an idea, e.g. a flag has symbolic meaning as the representation of a country

totalitarian a situation where the state holds total control over its citizens

tripling grouping points in threes

verbal irony when someone says the opposite of what they mean/intend (e.g. 'What a lovely day' when it's pouring with rain)

Wall Street crash a devastating stock market crash in 1929, which signalled the beginning of the Great Depression

OXFORD
UNIVERSITY PRESS

Great Clarendon Street, Oxford, OX2 6DP, United Kingdom

Oxford University Press is a department of the University of Oxford.

It furthers the University's objective of excellence in research, scholarship, and education by publishing worldwide. Oxford is a registered trade mark of Oxford University Press in the UK and in certain other countries

British Library Cataloguing in Publication Data

Data available

ISBN 978-019-830483-8

10 9 8 7 6 5 4 3 2 1

Printed in Great Britain by Bell and Bain Ltd., Glasgow

FSC MIX Paper from responsible sources FSC® C007785

Acknowledgements

The publisher and author are grateful for permission to reprint the following copyright material:

Extracts from *Animal Farm* by George Orwell (Penguin, 2008), copyright © George Orwell 1945, and extract from George Orwell's Preface to the Ukrainian edition of *Animal Farm* (Prometej, 1947), copyright © George Orwell 1947, reprinted by permission of A M Heath & Co Ltd, Authors' Agents, on behalf of Bill Hamilton as the Literary Executor of the Estate of the Late Sonia Brownell.

Extract from 'Animal Farm: Sixty Years On' by Robert Pearce in *History Today*, Vol 55, Issue 8, August 2005, reprinted by permission of History Today Ltd.

We have tried to trace and contact all copyright holders before publication. If notified, the publishers will be pleased to rectify any errors or omissions at the earliest opportunity.

The publisher and author would like to thank the following for permissions to use their photographs:

Cover: Leyn/Shutterstock; **p8:** AF archive/Alamy; AF archive/Alamy; **p14:** AF archive/Alamy; **p17:** AF archive/Alamy; **p20:** Halas & Batchelor Collection Ltd./The Bridgeman Art Library; **p26:** Everett Collection Historical/Alamy; **p28:** Rusig/Alamy; **p29:** Heritage Image Partnership Ltd/Alamy; **p30:** Danita Delimont/Alamy; **p33:** CORBIS; **p36:** Halas & Batchelor Collection Ltd./The Bridgeman Art Library; **p40:** Halas & Batchelor Collection Ltd./The Bridgeman Art Library; **p41:** Halas & Batchelor Collection Ltd./The Bridgeman Art Library; **p43:** AF archive/Alamy; **p44:** AF archive/Alamy; **p51:** Mila Atkovska/Shutterstock; **p54:** Moviestore collection Ltd/Alamy; **p57:** Bettmann/CORBIS; **p61:** Halas & Batchelor Collection Ltd./The Bridgeman Art Library; **p67:** Megapress/Alamy; **p70:** Moviestore collection Ltd/Alamy; **p74:** North Wind Picture Archives/Alamy